The Hundred Yard Lie

The Corruption of College Football and What We Can Do to Stop It

Rick Telander

With an Afterword by the Author
and Forewords by
Murray Sperber and Richard Warch

University of Illinois Press
Urbana and Chicago

For my friends at Sports Illustrated

Illini Books edition, 1996

Manufactured in the United States of America
P 5 4 3 2 1

This book is printed on acid-free paper.

Library of Congress Cataloging-in-Publication Data
Telander, Rick.
The hundred yard lie : the corruption of college football and what we can do to stop it / Rick Telander ; with an afterword by the author ; and forewords by Murray Sperber and Richard Warch. — Illini Books ed.
p. cm.
Originally published: New York : Simon and Schuster, c1989. With new forewords and afterword.
ISBN 0-252-06523-9 (pbk. : alk. paper)
1. Football—Corrupt practices—United States. 2. College sports—United States. I. Title.
GV959.T44 1996
796.332'63'0973—dc20 96-12412
CIP

Contents

Foreword

Murray Sperber

Rick Telander did much of the research for *The Hundred Yard Lie* in the late 1980s; however, a lifetime of playing football and thinking about sports preceded his work on the book. In his critique of college football, Telander does not skim along the surface; instead, he reveals an entire corrupt system—its genesis, present form, and future shape. Even though some of the coaches named in the book have bolted to other jobs and their annual incomes have increased to much larger amounts than noted here, *The Hundred Yard Lie* is as accurate today as when first published in 1989.

Telander knows football from the inside: he played in a tough Illinois high school league; he was an outstanding cornerback for Northwestern during one of its rare winning periods; and for many years he wrote about college football for *Sports Illustrated.* Contrary to the reaction of former Michigan coach Bo Schembechler—"Telander is a loser. He's been a loser all his life" (quoted in the *Chicago Tribune,* October 24, 1989)—the author has always been a winner, and his criticism of big-time college football is not a loser's whine but a winner's protest. Some of the most convincing and moving passages in the book occur in the interchapters, the author's stream-of-consciousness memories of the demons and fun of playing football. And the chapters on coaches—their pathology and limitations as well as his attachment to his Northwestern coach, Alex Agase—are revealing and poignant.

But the test of any book that tries to explain an entire social phenomemon is its predictive power. More than half a decade later, the reader can judge whether the critical matrix laid out by Telander accurately forecast what has occurred in college football and what will probably happen next. On the clairvoyant scale, *The Hundred Yard Lie* scores amazingly high. In 1989, the author hamered at the hypocrisy and cant of the NCAA, CFA, and member schools; since then, the velocity of their self-serving propaganda has accelerated, appearing ever more lame when excusing the scandal-of-the-week in college sports. He also predicted that among college athletes drug taking and weight training would increase significantly; subsequently, drug-masking techniques have become more sophisticated, steroid consumption continues unabated, and pumping iron occupies ever more hours of athletes' days—all of this despite the claims by the apologists for college sports that drug use has disappeared and that the players have plenty of time to attend class and to study.

Telander's most prescient remarks, however, concern the ongoing shift in the players' attitudes toward college sports. He describes some athletes as having "an intuitive sense about the hypocrisy of college ball. They see that everybody involved with the game—except those who actually play it—make money. So they stick their palms out and we label them mercenary or worse." Since 1989, many more athletes have caught on to the systemic hypocrisy of college sports and have begun to protest. Some have demanded their fair share of the revenue that they generate, a number of them in appearances before NCAA committees. This movement can only grow: as this book explains so well, big-time college sports are big-time entertainment—having nothing to do with the educational functions of the host universities—and as more athletes learn about the huge number of dollars rolling into athletic departments, their demands for a cut will intensify. (Telander also explains the massive inefficiency and corruption of most athletic departments and how, despite their considerable revenues, they manage to lose money and annually end up in the red.)

In pointing to this nexus between big-time sports entertainment and athletes' demands, Telander indicates the juncture at which college sports will forever change. Just as the 1994–95 professional baseball and hockey strikes were prolonged, in large part, by the players' realization that *they are the game*—not the fat-cat owners, corporations, front offices, and on-field personnel, who are interchangeable with other fat-cat owners, corporations, and so on—college athletes will come to realize, because increasingly they identify with the pros, that *they are the college game*—not the interchangeable universities, athletic departments, coaches, and so on—and they will act accordingly.

The conclusion to *The Hundred Yard Lie*—the author's proposal to professionalize big-time college football—makes perfect sense. When first published, this twenty-eight point plan, including the concept that schools choosing not to professionalize should return intercollegiate football to the real students and wind down their huge athletic departments, sparked controversy and widespread opposition. Now, only a paid propagandist for the NCAA could argue against his sensible and fair-minded ideas about "what we can do to stop" the corruption in college football. Unfortunately, the professionalization of big-time college sports will not occur without a struggle—as Telander explains, the college athletic establishment has a huge stake in the status quo—but his analysis indicates that this struggle will come, possible sooner than he foresaw.

In a number of passages, Telander vows that *The Hundred Yard Lie* would be his final word on college football, that he would never write about the subject again: "after everything's said [in this book] I'm gone." Fortunately for true fans, he continued to write about the game for *Sports Illustrated* until 1995, and now he keeps at it as a featured columnist for the *Chicago Sun-Times.*

Telander once described himself as a "truth-seeker and human speed-bump in front of runaway athletic departments everywhere." With the re-issue of *The Hundred Yard Lie,* he has built up his speed-bump, perhaps high enough to tear the weak underbelly of big-time college football and help bring about real reform. Every person with authority over intercollegiate athletics, particularly college presidents and trustees, should read *The Hundred Yard Lie* and use it as a guide to new rules for college sports, regulations that will actually benefit the athletes and the universities.

Foreword

Richard Warch

It has been seven years since publication of *The Hundred Yard Lie* and the chicken still has not grown lips. Which is but a shorthand way of saying that the condition of big-time college football that Rick Telander described in 1989 is pretty much unaltered. It would be wonderful to be able to point to the changes wrought to reverse what Telander called the corruption of college football, but almost all the evidence points in the other direction. Reissuing *The Hundred Yard Lie* therefore serves as a reminder to all who care about intercollegiate athletics that the work of reform is yet to be accomplished.

There has been some activity on the reform front, to be sure, most notably the Knight Commission Report of 1993 and the persistence and legislative successes of the Presidents Commission within the NCAA. One might plausibly argue that, given the long history of abuse in college sports, it may be too early to reach a verdict on their eventual impact. But even with greater public attention to and concern about the problems with Division I football—attention that Telander's book contributed significantly to arousing—alarming examples of excess and malfeasance routinely appear on local and national sports pages. In the face of these ongoing scandals, reform efforts often have the appearance of rearranging the deck chairs on the *Titanic*.

Perhaps the principal virtue of *The Hundred Yard Lie* is that it offers a litany of such scandals, the sheer volume of which leads the reader to Telander's conclusion: the problems demand more than a tinkering fix. He views the present condition of big-time college football as being beyond redemption, which is to say that he accepts what it has become: big-time entertainment, divorced from the mission of the sponsoring institution, and at its highest level "too bizarre and too dangerous to serve any educational function." The game has become, in short, what former University of Cincinnati coach Tony Mason alleged: "90 percent of the colleges are abiding by the rules, doing things right. The other 10 percent, they're going to bowl games." On one level, Telander's solution is to accept that condition—or something close to it—and let that other 10 percent create what amounts to a professional age-group league, pay its players, who need not be students, and receive subsidies from the NFL. Telander also has a set of proposed rules for schools that continue to play "college football," but he effectively divorces the 10 percent from the 90 percent, thereby eliminating the temptations and causes of fraud, corruption, and violations of NCAA rules and regulations.

Not everyone will agree with his solutions. But one sign that some of his proposals are gaining a following is the resistance they face, particularly his proposition that players be compensated for their services. To those who argue that football players are, after all, receiving a free higher education, perhaps one need only quote the immortal words of University of Virginia coach Sonny Randle: "We've stopped recruiting young men who want to come here to be students first and athletes second."

Once the proposal to pay players in the so-called Age-Group Professional Football League is accepted, the rest of Telander's recommendations fall into place almost naturally. They certainly run counter to long-held ideals regarding amateurism, student-athletes, and the glories of playing for dear old alma mater, which Telander reserves for the true college football teams. Those illusions, as Telander would call them, die hard. But to discover why he thinks they ought to be put to rest, one needs to read the analysis that leads him to that conclusion. Having done so, even the most devoted fan will find that college football will never appear quite the same again.

STRETCHING

There was always the grass.

He made sure to get his nose as close to it as he could during stretching, as close as the face mask let him. Players were arranged in formation at the start of practice, side by side in lines spaced ten yards apart like human yard stripes, grunting as they elongated the muscle fibers that had been bruised and contracted in earlier practices. Coaches roamed between the lines, clapping their hands, exhorting, occasionally stopping to join in and stretch some of their own aging tissue. There was a sweet dullness to it all, a mindlessness like the moment before dreaming. Somebody yelled, "Other leg," and there would be the shifting of bodies followed by low grumbling and sighs; then, "On your backs," and more shifting and groaning; then finally, "On your stomachs."

Now he would look into the grass. On days like this, when the sun was just so, he went into it. He weaved into the green canes like an explorer through a jungle, everything precise and brilliant in shades of emerald and purple and then brown where the tips of each blade had been cut by the lawn mower, but which now were the points on trees, on shields, on obelisks. It occurred to him that he had spent a lot of his young life around grass and soil. Just the smell of the stuff could revive him, make him travel. Sometimes he would encounter an insect in the depths of the grass, an aphid or leafhopper or a mite so tiny he couldn't believe God even knew it existed. But it was huge to him as he journeyed. He saw spores. Egg sacs. Fuzz. Fresh boulders of dirt made by a worm. Dewdrop chandeliers. He would drift, and sometimes he had moments of clarity like little sunbursts.

"Necks," a coach said, and he had to rise up on all fours out of the grass and wait for his partner to come over and put his leg out for him to push his helmet against. "Your neck'd make a nice pencil," his partner would say. He'd relax for a moment, lull his partner into thinking he hadn't heard, then push with all his might against his partner's leg and maybe get him to stumble sideways, maybe catch the coach's eye. His partner would come back from getting pushed, put his leg out, and they'd do the other side of the player's neck. His partner would cautiously take off his own chinstrap and furtively whack him on the helmet. To the world it was a small sound; inside the helmet it was the Liberty Bell cracking.

The coach would come by, his face grim as death. "Get serious!" he'd hiss to both players. Then he'd move on.

The player would continue his neck-building silently.

I am serious, he would want to say. You can't believe how goddamn serious I am.

CHAPTER 1

You Can't Let a Few Isolated Incidents Ruin the Sport for You

It was sometime early last season—I don't remember when exactly, but it was back before Jerry Parks shot Zarek Peters in Bud Hall, before my Sooner buddy Charles Thompson sold blow to the FBI agent, before Notre Dame taunted West Virginia in the Fiesta Bowl or Mike Stonebreaker got drunk and drove off the road and almost killed himself and his girlfriend, before a lot of the Hart Lee Dykes stuff got out or all the crap at Colorado and South Carolina and Oklahoma State made the news, before the Proposition 42 controversy, before I asked Florida State's "Neon" Deion Sanders what it was all about and he said, "Money," and even before the NCAA's $1.75-million report on athletes came out and Martin Massengale, the chairman of the NCAA Presidents' Commission, told us that all big-time college sport needs is a little "fine-tuning"—that I started to lose it.

I was talking with Steve Robinson on the phone and it just sort of welled over me. Steve is a good guy, the college football editor at *Sports Illustrated* where I am the Senior Writer on the college football beat. Steve came over from *Life* where he used to write and where he earned a reputation for being an honest, hardworking journalist. Steve and I are in touch almost daily during the season. I call him or he calls me and we bat things around. We yell and get vehement sometimes, though mostly it's me who does that, and we figure out what we think by hearing our ideas formed into words and questioned by the other person. It's a good process. I pity those poor writers who can't talk to their editors. But on this day I felt lost.

"What is it?" Steve asked.

I couldn't put my finger on it at first. My brain was like a computer screen that had gone haywire, words and gibberish streaming across it without control. A phrase kept whirring past: "child abuse." But who were the children? Football players? Us? How did this fit? What was the big deal—I'm a sportswriter, so I should just get out there and write about sports, in this case, college football. Get your assignment, Telander, shut up and get out there. But my mind was reeling. I have kids and I couldn't get this notion of child abuse out of my mind, about how football athletes are just kids going off to college to play ball, and how they're like my little kids, who seem so vulnerable, whom I want to protect from the ugliness of the world more than anything else, but who always seem to end up in the hands of other people, being taught lessons I don't believe in, receiving pain that does not need to be received. What is happening to our college football players? I asked Steve Robinson. Bad things are happening to them, I answered. To all of us. To fans, to students, to the fabric of the United States. Myths are being perpetuated in college football. People are lying in college football; blind, malicious people are protecting their butts at a tremendous psychic and societal cost. Something is so wrong here, I told Steve, that I don't think I can go on writing about the games and scores and strategies feeling what I feel, knowing what I know.

And I knew things. That was the problem. I *knew.* I had

material all over my office in Chicago, piles of information—books, clippings, quotes, scrawlings, jotted insights of varying perceptiveness and naivete, statistics, brochures, studies, charts, letters and notes that I'd been collecting for years, poems, photos, aphorisms, headlines, dumbbells, even my own college helmet with its cracking leather cheek pads and a couple of footballs that I sometimes just held for the hell of it—that combined to tell me what I felt: big-time college football is out of control, rotten from the foundation up. Was it always? Maybe, maybe not. But it was now, and that's all that mattered.

My thinking process and this excess of stimuli had suddenly reached critical mass. I thought of the time a few years ago in Key West when I cut my knee on a rusty trailer as I helped winch a Boston whaler out of the ocean. I didn't think anything of it. The small cut hardly bled at all. I rinsed it with seawater and went on about my business. Four nights later, my knee started to feel tight. Then it got hot. It was swelling. It seemed to expand as I looked at it, but I couldn't figure out why. The cut on my knee was now a tiny, healing scab off to the side of the affected area. But within an hour I could barely walk and my knee was red, huge, and throbbing. In agony I went to the hospital, and the doctor said that the staphylococci bacteria in the cut had moved around, found a favorable beachhead, and started expanding. Geometric progression being what it is, the platoon of germs had needed a little over a hundred hours to become an army. Now they were ready to raise hell. If this had been the Wild West, I would have asked the doctor to saw my leg off. And now as I talked on the phone with Steve Robinson, my brain felt the same way. Maybe he could saw my head off.

But Steve understood what I was saying, at least every now and then he acknowledged what I was getting at, agreeing, making his own points, reminding me that we had come to a lot of this revelatory stuff together, which soothed me. I was running a wildfire rap on him that was close to stream-of-consciousness blathering with points going all the way back to ancient Rome and on through history to the discovery of America and the introduction of slavery and the Civil War and the industrial revolution and Victorian England and the rise of the leisure class and Teddy Roosevelt and sneaky guys like George Gipp and Knute Rockne and the influence of machismo and the pioneering spirit combined with nostalgia and the romantic historical revision of certain influential writers and nuclear capability and of course, cash, and all the ways these disparate elements affected—nay, created—this mess we call college football. As I mentioned, I wasn't being real clear. But I certainly was laying out some passion. All of a sudden I just knew. It was not a good feeling. It was more like getting kicked in the head and waking up and understanding precisely what your previously incomprehensible IRS form says and realizing at the same time that you owe a bucketful of money.

But it was, too, a relief. I finally had it all together. I know, I kept thinking to myself. I know. And what I knew was that high-level college football—the big-time stuff—was corrupt. And I knew how and why. All the little pieces were finally forming a whole. Hypocrisy, commercialism, amateurism, and a bunch of other "isms" were the parts to the puzzle, and I was going to put the whole damn thing together and show people what it looked like.

This was, as I have stated, before the season was far along; if I had known what was yet to come, I might have exploded on the spot. It was after South Carolina nosetackle Tommy Chaikin lost his mind to steroids and put the .357 magnum under his chin, and former Wisconsin Stevens-Point star Keith Majors hung himself in a northern-Wisconsin county jail after leading his team to a tie for the 1987 NAIA championship (they cut him down before he died), but it was before the three players got arrested for gang rape at Oklahoma or the players at Prairie View A & I boycotted their program en masse because they claimed head coach Haney Catchings was brutal and withheld schoolbooks from them if they didn't play well, and it was before Benji Ramirez's heart exploded in Ashtabula and before I got the letter from Syracuse coach Dick MacPherson telling me to please "as a writer, don't feel compelled to sometimes overreact to college abuses of athletes. Remember sometimes the athlete is also guilty of misuse of his talents and gifts, which reflects poorly on all." I thought about that for a while, and of course, the coach is right—the child abuse can go the other way, too—kids who have lost their ethical way or who never had any ethics to begin with can just work over befuddled, insensitive, old-fashioned adults. And then, as if in response to MacPherson's letter, a few days later Syracuse basketball forward Derrick Coleman and football players Al Glover and Cal Ingram were involved in a fight outside a fraternity party that led to Coleman's being arrested and charged with harassment and criminal mischief, while Glover and Ingram had the incident and their violation of university regulations noted on their school records. Child abuse was on my mind, but the notion expanded until it became something like abuse, generally, with victims everywhere.

Oh, the arrests and transgressions. Those were the things that got me going. Steve used to come into his office after the weekend and read the accumulated college football wire-service stuff to me over the phone. Rapes, burglaries, assaults, drug-dealing, drunkenness, bizarre stuff, things that silenced both of us. At Georgia Tech a 6′7″, 321-pound offensive tackle named Mike Mooney and his football buddy, Kevin Salisbury 6′4″, 245 pounds, beat up three people in a pizza joint, including an undercover cop and a 5′8″, 120-pound female architecture student who was going to need plastic surgery to fix her face. There must have been a full moon out that night, January 17, 1989, because just down the road at Clemson two football Tigers beat up a student in the rest room of a bar, breaking his jaw and cutting him up pretty good. Both players got out on $5,000 bonds. Right around that same time at Colorado, running back O. C. Oliver was arrested for failing to appear in court on a traffic violation, defensive tackle Stephen Cole Hayes was arrested for investigation of shoplifting (and subsequently found to have an outstanding warrant for failure to appear on a traffic violation), running back Marcus Reliford was arrested (though later acquitted) for the alleged rape of an eighteen-year-old woman after entering her dormitory room through a window, and two other players were arrested for participating in a brawl outside a Boulder tavern. Oh, and there was another Colorado arrest that same week—a U.C. player was picked up on suspicion of torturing, killing, and skinning a pet rabbit. Neither Steve nor I were sure what law guaranteed the safety of pets, but it seemed insignificant when we considered that in the last three years over two dozen other Buffalos had been arrested for crimes ranging from trespassing to serial rape.

The troubles football players were getting into were a big catalyst for my brainfire. But they weren't the sole cause. Anybody with one eye open could see that there was rottenness throughout the realm, on a variety of levels. Certainly, the win-at-all-costs mentality had a lot to do with the increase in subhuman behavior of some college athletes. Former Colorado split end Loy Alexander, the team's leading receiver in 1983, declared after the Buffs finished 1-10 in 1984 that he was tired of being surrounded by teammates of impeccable character and zero talent. "We've got enough altar boys," he said. "We need some athletes." Presto, Coach Bill McCartney recruited some "athletes," the team has finished 7-4 and 8-4 the last two seasons, and no priests are searching the Colorado locker rooms for helpers.

But lesser sins have left their stain as well. As I write this, there are seventeen schools on NCAA probation for a host of violations in a variety of sports. Most of the transgressions have to do with your run-of-the-mill corruption and the failure to follow established recruiting guidelines by coaches and boosters. Under-the-table money given to athletes, ticket-scalping, phony entrance exams, doctored transcripts, clandestine recruiting visits—things like that. It is stuff that has been going on since the NCAA formed back in 1906 and will be going on as long as the NCAA exists. Why the hell should anything change? When an entire organization is built on hypocrisy and exploitation, as college football is, you damn near *hope* there is continuing trouble, just to prove that people are still breathing and alert. But the transgressions make a mockery of any ethical standards the schools might profess to endorse. Five of the eight Southwest Conference football programs (and one basketball program) have gone on NCAA probation since 1985, with Southern Methodist University just finishing up its "death penalty"—the total suspension of the football program for three years—for having a regime so corrupt that the governor of Texas was moved to say that even with probation it didn't seem fair to quit making illicit payments to the athletes now that the fellows had come to count on the cash so much. And the beauty of all this is that the SWC was formed in 1914 with the stated purpose of promoting ethical standards among member institutions.

But all NCAA violations are just that, violations of arbitrary rules established by the members of the organization to help police those same members. Sort of like the bylaws for the Boy Scouts or Knights of Columbus. None of the NCAA "illegalities" are acts that are against the law. They are not crimes, only breaches of rules of the game known as college sport. If you're a quarterback and you get videotaped selling seventeen grams of cocaine for $1,400 to an undercover narcotics agent, like, say, Charles Thompson did, then you may be in big trouble with the law but not with the NCAA. Oklahoma went on its current three-year probation not for drug dealings or rapes or shootings, but for, among other things, getting "involved in a 'bidding war' for a highly recruited prospective student-athlete," and for obtaining "a round-trip airline ticket at a travel agency in Norman on the same day (another) player asked for a ticket in order to travel home for his grandmother's funeral," according to the NCAA Committee on Infractions.

No, if it had just been athlete crime that did me in, I would have gotten out long ago. It was the sheer volume of all kinds of things going on in college football that overwhelmed me: the criminal behavior, the rampant pursuit of money, the tunnel vision of the coaches, the complacency of the fans, the sliminess of the boosters, the sanctimonious platitudes of the NCAA brass, the exploitation of the players, the desire to expand the season, to televise everything, to make money, money, money, the brutality and taunting on the field itself, the absurdity of the "student athlete" notion, the lack of anything remotely like an ethical anchor holding these programs and their patrons to the ground—that filled me with disgust. And the ugliest part of all was that these sins were being committed in a world that we have always assumed to be a realm of virtue and idealism. If colleges aren't pure in America, and if the things that take place in their classrooms and dorms and stadiums aren't good, then what can we have faith in?

I asked Steve that. I may or may not have given him time to respond. I think I babbled on.

After a while I stopped, I know that. The bottom line, Steve said, was that he wanted me to ride out the season and see if things didn't get better. In truth, I wanted to, also. What would it be like trying to write about this sport now that I had the goods on it? How would I judge things? I wouldn't, I told myself. I would simply let the season flow and I would ride it like a kid on a surfboard. One last wave. At the end, I'd hang ten and paddle ashore.

If I'd known how nuts the season was going to turn out, I would have kicked out right on the spot. But I made it through, and now I'm out of here. I'm gone. As soon as this book is done, I'm turning in my badge. Mark Mulvoy, the managing editor of *Sports Illustrated,* knows how I feel. And so does Peter Carry, the executive editor. He called me to the New York office to talk about it as part of our normal year-end review, and he nodded when I told him how I felt. "Take some time," Peter said. "Think about another sport." This was just after the Fiesta Bowl and right before the kid from Notre Dame, Bob Satterfield, died mysteriously in a South Bend night club just hours after shaking hands with President Reagan at the White House with the rest of the number one–ranked Irish. And it was a couple weeks before South Carolina coach Joe Morrison checked out at age fifty-one and a reporter from somewhere called me up and wondered aloud if the story I'd written with Tommy Chaikin about all the goddamn steroids used at S.C. had caused the stress that had helped blow apart Morrison's heart.

Peter said, "Take your time, don't rush it." I wasn't going to quit *S.I.* I still believe in the beauty of sport, the transcendence of games. So I've been thinking hard about what I can move to, and one sport that comes to mind is boxing. Start at the bottom and there's nowhere to go but up.

But I have thought often about the words of New York University chancellor Dr. L. Jay Oliva, who wrote not long ago in the *New York Times,* "I am mystified, angered and shamed by the current state of college athletics in the United States." How, I wonder, can anyone not be? When I was camped out in Norman for a couple weeks in February, raking the muck on the Sooners, I felt myself feeling so damn sorry for all the players who were in trouble, deep trouble, that I dreaded actually reporting the facts. Maybe they didn't even think they were doing anything wrong when they committed their crimes. Maybe they were so trapped in a moral vacuum that they were looking for something, anything, to give them some boundaries. Rape. You hate to say it, but what is it other than violent domination, sort of like the worst of football itself? "You can't blame the athlete when he sees the whole world cheating," says Dr. Thomas Tutko, a professor of sports psychology at San Jose State University, addressing the issue of athletic crime. "That seems to be the ethos in our society today: 'Can I get away with it?' is the question. Athletes don't feel they're doing anything wrong."

That is tragic. Particularly when you couple it with the spoutings of the NCAA officials. At a recent seminar NCAA executive director Dick Schultz said, "If you ask the average person what his perception of college athletics is, he'll tell you four things: Colleges make millions of dollars at the expense of the college athlete; all coaches cheat; athletes never graduate; and all athletes are drug addicts."

Schultz then gave reasons why those perceptions are not true. But I can tell you what I think, what I know. The big-time universities *do* generate millions at the expense of the athletes—Michigan's football team, for instance, pulls in at least $12 million; I can't list all the coaches caught cheating in the last fifty years because I don't want this book to look like a phone directory, but consider, if you will, that in a recent survey of 66 of the 104 Division 1-A head coaches by the *Rocky Mountain News* of Denver, 41 of the coaches themselves thought their peers cheated; 70 percent of the players in the NFL have not graduated from college; the amount of drugs—from steroids to marijuana to cocaine to alcohol—used by football players is, at least on some teams, way out of control.

Most of what I'm saying here is old hat. Nothing new under the sun. Listen to the opening comments made by Lawrence University president Richard Warch at the NCAA special convention in Dallas, June 29, 1987: "A government report laments the professionalism that has brought 'discredit upon college sports.' An American president decries the 'sensationalism and hysteria' that afflict intercollegiate athletics. A national education association meeting hears a speech on the 'serious evils of college athletics.' A major educational foundation issues a report on the state of American college sports—and finds it troubled. And a university president lambasts the 'injustice, hypocrisy, and fraud' of big-time football. Familiar stuff? Of course. Except that these five events occurred in 1885, 1905, 1915, 1929, and 1950. Ladies and gentlemen, we have been here before."

Oh, haven't we. The past is the present, but more so, because now we have the added pressure of drugs, racial exploitation, and TV. Warch—and we'll hear more from him later—suggests taking all television, bowl, and postseason revenues from the few successful football teams and distributing the money to all the NCAA member organizations on an "enrollment formula" basis. This, he reasons, will "abolish the extrinsic rewards of huge financial bonuses and use the money to support the programs of *all* institutions that field athletic teams as a part and expression of their educational process." Nice thought, and Warch is a nice man (we have spent much time together discussing our views on athletics), but his proposal is as likely to gain support as a chicken is to grow lips. "Hellfire!" I can hear the assorted AD's screaming. "That's communism!"

What it is, is dreaming, but it at least addresses the cash-cow status of big-time football. Money, received for providing vicarious thrills to viewers, is what drives college football these days. "Sport is no longer a vehicle to create character change," says James H. Frey, a sociology professor at the University of Nevada–Las Vegas and the president of the North American Society for the Sociology of Sport. "It's an entertainment vehicle."

It seems everybody around the sport—except those directly involved with it: athletic directors, coaches, flunkies, boosters, and all the assorted yahoos who hang around and dress their kids in State Tech cheerleading/football outfits—seems to understand this. *Atlanta Constitution* columnist Lewis Grizzard suggests that a new college major might end the fraud of football players masquerading as real students: "We give Lorenzo Linebacker a scholarship and allow him to major in football. He learns to play football, goes to daily classes to learn how to fill them with air, how to make one, how to coach others in the game, and even how to sell a football. . . . Lorenzo gets his degree in football. Maybe he can go and play in the pros and make millions of dollars. Or maybe he can become a coach. Or maybe he can get a job in a sporting-goods store. Either way, it's better than what he could have had otherwise. It's silly to offer a degree in football? I had a friend from high school who majored in music at college, learned to play guitar, and was last seen doing five nights a week in a Holiday Inn lounge. Life could turn out that way for Lorenzo, too, if we just give him a chance."

Well, I have my own proposals for cleaning up the mess, but you don't get them until the end of this book, and by then you may be so sick of the whole thing that you just want to take up fishing. But put yourself in my shoes for a moment. How would you feel if you confronted the president of a major university, asked him about the recent crimes committed by his football team, and the man dismissed the actions by calling them "isolated incidents"? That's what I asked Oklahoma's interim president David Swank, the former dean of the OU Law School, and that's how he responded. For a second I thought, jeez, maybe the guy is right, maybe I'm overreacting. Then I remembered I was asking this bespectacled professor of jurisprudence about three alleged rapes, a drug bust, and a shooting; and I recalled that Jerry Parks's bullet had missed his teammate's heart by three inches, and that Parks had then pointed the gun at his own head and allegedly pulled the trigger, but the gun misfired. So, except for the intervention of blind luck, there would have been a murder and suicide to go along with the other felonies. And it all happened in just twenty-five days. Isolated incidents? Dean of the law school? The Twilight Zone?

What you find as you go through life is that people can believe in anything they want, and that the strength of their belief is quite often in reverse order to the actual validity of the concept. We like to believe in things that make us feel good. A recent study shows that 71 percent of Americans believe in heaven, but only 53 percent believe in hell. I can understand that. I'd rather even fewer folks believed in hell, particularly if God made His decisions based on polls. But myths are so strong for us, fill such a need, that we care very little about their basis in fact. How about the story that at the 1936 Berlin Olympics

Adolf Hitler openly refused to shake 100-meter champion Jesse Owens's hand, foreshadowing the racial atrocities of the Third Reich? It's neatly symbolic and often printed as fact, but it never happened. Olympic historian Andrew Strenk, a former Olympic swimmer, lecturer at Southern Cal, and a man I spoke with at some length for this book, points out that on the day Owens won the 100 meters, no athletes at all were invited to Hitler's box. "It tarnishes the Olympics to base what we believe on falsehood," says Strenk.

And it tarnishes college football to believe some of the things we now take for granted. Freshman eligibility, for instance. Why have it? Who knows. It's terrible for eighteen-year-olds. But coaches like it. Why have spring practice? No reason again, except coaches like it. Players should always stay in school until they graduate, right? Why? If you had a million-dollar contract waiting for you in the pros, would *you* risk injury playing for free?

Last December I was in Tokyo with Oklahoma State running back Barry Sanders when he won the 1988 Heisman Trophy for being the best player in college football. OSU was preparing to play Texas Tech in something called the Coca-Cola Bowl, sponsored by guess who, and Sanders was distressed that he even had to show up at the CBS-TV studio on game day to receive his award via satellite linkup with the Downtown Athletic Club in New York City. A fourth-year junior at OSU with a year of eligibility left, Sanders didn't even want to consider leaving school for the NFL before his final season. He just wanted to play football, free of fanfare. His devotion to the rules he'd learned was almost laughable in its innocence. He hardly went out of his room during the week in Japan, preferring to rest and study. One day in the lobby of the Miyako Hotel he told me, "Japan is nice. The buildings are compact. The people are occupied with their jobs; they're pretty serious. But you know what the saying is, 'There's no place like home.' "

Right after that he approached Oklahoma State publicist Steve

Buzzard and said, "Steve, I understand there's supposed to be some *thing* on Sunday."

"Yes," said Buzzard. The thing was the Heisman Trophy ceremony.

"I really don't want to do it."

Coach Pat Jones and the rest of the OSU staff finally convinced Sanders to show up for the ritual—as an enticement they said he could take his fullback, Garrett Limbrick, and the entire offensive line along with him. Sanders brought the gang along, reluctantly accepted the award, then headed over to the Tokyo Dome where he proceeded to rush for 357 yards in as remarkable a display of running as this *gaijin* reporter has ever seen.

For the season, Sanders finished with 2,628 rushing yards, a 238.9 yards-per-game average, 39 touchdowns, and 3,249 all-purpose yards, all new NCAA records. And now despite the fact that his whole offensive line was graduating and his school was soon to go on NCAA probation for three years—no TV, no bowl games, reduced scholarships—and that at 5′8″, 198 pounds of rock-solid muscle Sanders was unlikely ever to be in better shape, he insisted he shouldn't turn to the pros. Even though that was where he truly wanted to be.

Ironically, closely watching Sanders in his torment was teammate Hart Lee Dykes, the all-American wide receiver and Typhoid Mary of college ball. Dykes was the kid whose testimony to the NCAA regarding recruiting violations, granted in exchange for personal immunity to charges, had helped place four schools—Texas A&M, Oklahoma, Illinois, and now even his own Oklahoma State—on probation. If Sanders was the Mr. Naive of college ball, Dykes was its Mr. Capitalist.

"The Heisman," Dykes said sadly in the locker room after the Coca-Cola Bowl. "I know *I'd* be able to deal with the thing."

Eventually, Sanders would indeed come out of school "early"—that is, before his coaches, fans, and the NCAA and NFL officials wanted him to—to play football for a living. But his reluctance to do anything against the system only underlined how much the system uses a kid like him. ''Greedy'' players like Dykes, on the other hand, have an intuitive sense about the hypocrisy of college ball. They see that everybody involved with the game—except those who actually play it—make money. So they stick their palms out, and we label them mercenary or worse.

Playing in the NFL is clearly the goal of many college players; the colleges are just as clearly the minor league for the NFL. What Barry Sanders believed in is the myth that college football is still just a simple kid's game. Wouldn't that be nice if it were true? But if it were, we wouldn't have erected so many shrines to the program. Shrines such as the $3 million, 16,000-square-foot Paul W. Bryant Museum in Tuscaloosa, which was dedicated last fall to ''house the history of Alabama football, with special emphasis on the legendary coach.'' Shrines such as Michigan Stadium in Ann Arbor, which holds 101,701, and when full (attendance has topped 100,000 for eighty-five straight home games, dating back to October 1975) generates enough capital to make the down payment on, say, a new General Motors auto plant. Shrines such as Oklahoma's Bud Wilkinson Hall, which lies in the shadow of its parent shrine, Owen Field, the greensward (green carpet, actually) where an entire state fulfills itself on Sooner Saturdays.

''In other cultures, stimulation of the imagination in the direction of noble feelings stems most often from historical heroes and traditional folkways,'' writes Leonard Koppett in *Sports Illusion, Sports Reality*, a treatise on sports mythology. ''In twentieth-century America, spectator sports serve this function . . .'' Yes, they do.

Leafing through some old clippings I have stacked on my desk, I come to one from an article written by Allen Guttmann, a professor of American Studies at Amherst College: ''Chariot races in Constantinople in 532 touched off the worst sports riot in history. When the fans of the 'blues' and fans of the 'greens' were finally subdued by Justinian's army, 30,000 people were dead.''

I find myself wondering if the blues and greens themselves got off the oval safely, if they ducked into a tunnel guarded by stadium police and ran like hell to their dressing rooms or bolted outside to their horses or camels or whatever they had tethered nearby and just rode like the wind for home. People have always made a bigger deal out of sports than perhaps they should have. I guess I do, too. But then, reporting on college football is what I do for a living. And I get mad when I sense hypocrisy, which I sense all over the place in this thing.

George Bush's office calls Barry Sanders at Oklahoma State and invites him to the presidential inauguration. Sanders declines, shocking the President-elect's people, saying he doesn't want to miss his classes. It's such a marvelous gesture—take that all you phony bastards who just assume I'm a minor leaguer waiting to be called up!—that it seems wasted on mere politicians. In fact, it's such a naive gesture (nobody in the NFL is ever going to ask if you have a degree, Barry) that it's pretty much wasted on everybody.

That's why I didn't go to this year's special NCAA get-together in Kansas City, the one thrown by the NCAA for selected association officials, football coaches, athletic directors, and journalists. I felt it would be a wasted trip. I went last year and barely kept my temper while listening to the presentations from Dick Schultz and various good-ole-boy coaches, explaining why college players should not be allowed to leave school early for the NFL, why everything was hunky-dory, etc. This year, with my accompanying brainfire, I know I would have ended up in a fistfight with somebody—who knows whom, maybe Schultz himself, but probably with some rasping geezer who said I looked like a hippie or a wimp or riled me in some other mundane way. Because I'm wired tight right now. I'm ornery. And America itself is still very intense about this game.

I find it telling that during the 1985 $50-million *Ariel Sharon* v. *Time, Inc.* libel trial, a suit that dealt with the responsibility and shame over the 1982 massacre of hundreds of Palestinians by Israeli-allied Lebanese Christians while Sharon was Israel's defense minister, the jury stopped its deliberations to watch the Super Bowl. With the eager jurors in another room, U.S. District Judge Abraham D. Sofaer asked lawyers for both sides, "I'm sure we're all in agreement the jurors will be permitted to watch the Super Bowl?"

"Absolutely," was the answer.

A year earlier, a lawyer in Columbus, Ohio, demanded a new trial for his client, who had been convicted of involuntary manslaughter, robbery, and drug charges by a jury that rushed its decision because the members wanted to watch the telecast of the Ohio State–Michigan game. A signed affidavit by one juror said he had been pressured into changing his vote from innocent to guilty by jurors who wanted to root, root, root for the Buckeyes. And just last November, the fans at Tiger Stadium in Baton Rouge reacted so wildly to LSU's fourth-quarter touchdown to upset Auburn, 7–6, that they set off a vibration that registered on the LSU geology department's intermediate period seismograph, an earthquake detector.

But for me, the word *abuse* won't go away. As far back as 1884 people had serious concerns about the college game and its place in the realm of higher learning. That year a committee of Harvard faculty investigated the game, and the members of the panel were appalled by the savage brutality of the players and the wanton bloodlust of the spectators. In 1905, a year in which there were twenty-three football deaths, the sport came as close as it ever has to being banned. Even Teddy Roosevelt, the Great White Hunter who believed in football's manly rigors and had once declared, "I have a hearty contempt for [a student] if he counts a broken arm or collarbone as of serious consequence when balanced against the chance of showing that he possesses hardihood, physical prowess, and courage," now had his doubts. Said Professor Shailer Mathews of the University of Chicago Divinity School, "From the President of the United States to the humblest member of a school and college faculty there arises a general protest against this boy-killing, man-mutilating, money-making, education-prostituting, gladiatorial sport."

Mathews's squawk had a nice ring to it, but it did not bring about the downfall of the sport. College representatives met and came up with some rules changes—the ten-yard rule for a first down and the forward pass, among others—to open up the game and avoid the hideous line-of-scrimmage scrums then in favor. In 1910 and 1912 more rules were added to liberate the game even more, and as the deaths and serious injuries caused by the sport went down, so, too, did the cry to abolish football. Basically, the coaches and ADs had pulled a slick one on the public and the universities. By making rules changes that made the game safer (though certainly not safe), they had also effectively killed protests about the game's ethics and its place on campus. Indeed, by the 1920s the complaints about college football became little more than a nuisance, part of the background din, a low-energy whining that came with the territory and that no one—probably not even the complainers themselves—expected would be acted upon.

Coaches and athletic directors and football-loving college presidents had seized upon the purported character-building effect of the game and used that as their bludgeon against public opinion: just tell everyone that football builds better men, and right away you've silenced all but your most effete critics. MIT president Francis A. Walker stated in 1893 that playing football demanded "courage, coolness, steadiness of nerve, quickness of apprehension, resourcefulness, self-knowledge, self-reliance" and developed "something akin to patriotism and public spirit." It's tough to argue against something so wonderfully formative; it's why coaches make the same arguments today when cornered by critics.

But the abuses still stand out. There remains the atavistic notion that college football players should be amateurs, content to labor simply for free educations, items that many players may not even want. ''Amateurism is evil in principle,'' says Leonard Koppett, and we'll find out why soon enough. And how are football players supposed to act as serious students, even if they want to be, when they are asked to put in twenty, thirty, forty, or more hours a week at their sport? Even such a staunch, regime-defending coach as Nebraska's Tom Osborne says, ''We're progressively asking more and more of the players and giving them less and less in return. I would hope that if something is done, some compensation could be given to the players.''

Along the way has come the total commercialization of the sport, with college athletic departments looking first and foremost to the bottom line when considering football's good and bad features. Corporate sponsorship makes the bowl games sound like objects from the mergers and acquisitions section of the business page—the Mobil Corporation Cotton Bowl, the Sunkist Fiesta Bowl, the John Hancock Sun Bowl, the Sea World Holiday Bowl, the USF&G Sugar Bowl, the Mazda Gator Bowl. Not that there's anything wrong with corporations—universities themselves are really nothing but corporations trying to make a go of it—but outside funding only makes it that much easier to sell out a little more, to give up a tad more integrity the next time around. Can corporate sponsorship of athletic dorms, double sessions, ankle-taping, and picture day be far behind?

High on the list of football problems is the influx of drugs, both legal and illegal, performance enhancing and recreational, as well as the new religion of weight-lifting as an all-consuming passion. TV has its obtrusive nose in this mess as well, as do the questionable ethics of coaches, alumni, and those reptilian things known as boosters. Mostly, though, the whole ugly affair sits on a cardhouse called hypocrisy, which is nothing more than something pretending to be that which it is not. You'll hear the word *hypocrisy* a lot in the course of this book. Hypocrisy is a nasty customer.

I was trying to think of some good aspects to big-time college football, and I did, though most of the points are predictably boring (which does not mean they aren't valuable, just that they're not very juicy) and somewhat personal. At any rate, the good things I came up with will not in any way detract from the vigor with which I plan to attack the system. They only prove that the system is salvageable and worthy of change, that you can't really get mad at something unless you love it a little bit.

I stumbled upon this guy Dale Coventry, saw his balding head in an article in the *Chicago Sun-Times*, and I began to have pangs of remorse. Ah, dear, dear football, why have I forsaken thee? Coventry is an assistant public defender in Chicago, and one day last winter in the Cook County Criminal Court Building, he spotted a young man bolting down a courtroom aisle. The young man, named Anthony Skipper, looked like a fleeing criminal, and indeed, people all around were screaming, "Stop him! Stop him!" So Coventry "gently pushed aside" Assistant Public Defender Joann Dineen, with whom he had been talking, dropped his briefcase, bulled his neck, and tackled Skipper as though the youth were a ballcarrier cutting for the end zone and Coventry were an aroused linebacker.

Skipper was, indeed, an escaping convict, and he had already run over Assistant State's Attorney James Bigoness, breaking the attorney's arm in the process. And the forty-five-year-old Coventry was, indeed, a former linebacker—Lawrence College class of '66—simply responding to a situation requiring immediate action.

"It was a good tackle," Coventry said after Skipper had been carted off by police and order had returned to the courthouse. "It all came back to me."

Coventry went on, "The guy would have been in big trouble if he had gotten any farther because the deputy sheriffs involved in security are big, tough dudes with guns." And it struck me that here was a noble, considerate, brave man using his football experience for the benefit of mankind. Why, he even spared the criminal himself from a worse fate!

"Clearly [Skipper] belonged in court, not running out of it, and I just happened to be there," concluded Coventry. I pictured him saying it with a timid shrug. The man was modest, too. Football needs such alumni, making tackles on bad guys all over this country, to help ward off the black cloud descending on the sport. But Lawrence plays Division III football these days, and Dale Coventry, I'm afraid, doesn't have much to do with the problems at the Division I level. And that's where the curtain is dropping. At any rate, it's high-level football I'm attacking, and no simple act of samaritanism is going to make me tiptoe away. This is a diatribe. As Lord Byron once said (I have envisioned him as a brooding, flamboyant, dissension-causing wide receiver had he not been born short and with a clubfoot some eighty-one years before football was invented), "In composition, I do not think second thoughts are best." I agree.

I've been asked how my disgust with big-time college football came to be, and all I can say is, it's a good question. Certainly, my last few years of covering the sport in depth for *Sports Illustrated* have given me the close observation needed to get really ticked off about something. But coverage is not the only factor. As my older sister once said to me when I was a kid bitching about some fact of daily life, "You know what you are, Rick?" "What?" I asked with a sneer. "Disgruntled," she replied, slamming the door.

I've also been called emotional and cynical and sarcastic. I like to think those things are all functions of perceptiveness. But how did this outrage come about, anyway? I'm reminded of a passage from Hemingway's *The Sun Also Rises* (Hem I see as a big-gutted guard prone to chop blocks and heat exhaustion) wherein Bill asks Mike, the dissolute party animal, how he went bankrupt.

"Two ways," Mike replies. "Gradually and then suddenly."

Me too, I guess. This has been building for some time, this indignation. Then it exploded. Nothing new under the sun.

At any rate, I'll give you the truth as I see it and a modest proposal for cleaning up college football. You can ignore what I'm saying or take it to heart. You can deal with it any way you want. But after everything's said and the cards are flat on the table, it's your hand. I'm gone.

STRETCHING

The playground was big and they could go anywhere they wanted in it during recess, as long as they didn't cause trouble. They played softball most of the time, or soccer, or chase.

One day two kids got into a fight and the smaller of the two hit the other one in the mouth. This fascinated him. There were seldom fights on the school playground—the grass itself seemed to soothe the children—and never had one boy hit another in the mouth. There was a small amount of blood, and the two were taken off to the principal's office. The kids talked about the fight for the rest of the day.

Sometimes the boys would kick around a red playground ball until they got bored. Then someone would pick up the ball and throw it to somebody else. The ball would go around that way for a while, then get dropped and someone would kick it, then there would be a scramble for the ball and maybe a pileup with one boy coming away with the ball. The ballcarrier would grin and either throw the ball to somebody else or try to run away. Someone would grab him by the arm or neck and try to drag him down. There would be another pileup.

Occasionally there would be a small amount of blood, but nobody cared. The boys had invented a game.

But roughhousing was not allowed during recess, and if the teachers saw the boys acting like savages, the boys were in trouble. So they would go off to the far edge of the playground, behind some trees, and play this thing they called Slaughter, which was short for Slaughter the Man with the Ball, which was the name they had come up with spontaneously for their game.

But if the teachers saw them, they were in big trouble. So they'd hide and play and get caught and then serve their time. Sometimes they had to write things on the blackboard. Sometimes just stand somewhere.

But they didn't stop playing. This was too much fun. This was something.

CHAPTER 2

Playing for Free Is Noble

When Chicago Bears safety Maurice Douglass missed one of the afternoon pickup basketball games at the Multiplex gym in suburban Chicago recently, it suddenly dawned on me where he was: He was testifying in the Norby Walters–Lloyd Bloom trial down at the United States District Court on South Dearborn.

Quite a few of the Bears play over at the Multiplex during the off-season, and since I'm a basketball junkie who belongs to the same gym and I play hoops anytime I can, I have a lot of contact with the guys. Since I'm of generic defensive-back size, some days I have to guard Ron Morris, the Bears' wide receiver from Southern Methodist; some days I guard Douglass, who played at Kentucky; and on some days—before he was waived—I covered safety Egypt Allen, "The Egyptian," from Texas Christian. Douglass, Morris, and Allen all were victims of—or perhaps co-conspirators with, or users of, depending on your interpretation—Walters and Bloom, two sports agents put on trial for signing numerous college athletes to professional contracts before their amateur eligibility expired and then using strong-arm tactics to keep the players as clients. Walters and Bloom were also charged with defrauding seven universities out of the athletes' sports scholarships and with invoking the name of reputed New York mobster Michael Franzese in an unsuccessful attempt to take over a concert tour by the Jackson Five.

But more significant than the seven counts of racketeering, conspiracy, and mail fraud against Walters and Bloom, at least as far as the college football world is concerned, are the stories that the testifying players told about their respective schools and, by implication, the NCAA and the entire hypocritical world of amateur collegiate sport. Mo Douglass, also known as The Stripper because of his off-season work as a male clothes-peeler for partying women, sat on the stand in his cream-colored jacket, white silk shirt, and silver-tipped snakeskin cowboy boots and explained what it was like for him when Walters spread out $2,500 in cash and said it was Douglass's if he signed with him and Bloom.

"I didn't go there to sign, but when they put the money in front of me, I took it," Douglass said. "When you put twenty-five hundred dollars out in front of any college kid, he'd take it."

Well, Mo, maybe that's true, maybe it isn't. Certainly, it is more likely to occur when the college kid is a black football star from a poor background without a strong father figure at home, as was the case with most of the athletes recruited by Walters and Bloom. Indeed, the fifty-eight-year-old Bloom, who was already a successful manager of several black singing groups, went after good black players who could easily be influenced by the agent's glib, flashy, pseudo-soulful sales pitch. Between games one day at the gym, I asked Douglass if Walters had impressed him with anything in particular.

"Yeah, he introduced me to the New Edition," Douglass said. "They were his band. He seemed for real."

When Douglass later told Bloom he was going with another agent, Jim Steiner of St. Louis, Bloom was not as cheerful as at the first meeting.

"He told me if I didn't return the money and the cars, he'd have somebody break my legs," Douglass told the court.

Each of the athletes who testified in the six-week trial repeated or embellished Douglass's tale of being impressed by these fast-talking agents who offered them money in return for doing something they had been told was unethical: signing a contract for representation in the National Football League while the athletes were supposedly still amateurs. Not every player was threatened with a leg-breaking if he welshed on his contract—though Ron Morris also was—but each implied that taking the money from the agents seemed reasonable at the time, regardless of the risk to his amateur career or conflict with his conscience. The pathetic part about the whole affair is that Walters, though clearly a con man of the first order, was also something of a victim himself, an opportunistic (if threatening) businessman simply trying to cash in on what looked to him like a good deal: signing poor, talented kids who craved money and would earn it soon enough in the NFL but were denied it during their college careers by repressive NCAA rules. To Walters, the players were entertainers, pure and simple. "No difference," he said. "A sports star is a rock star. They're all the same."

The thing he didn't anticipate was the vehemence with which the NCAA and college football lords would deny that parallel. With his brazen cockiness and rock-and-roll chutzpah, Walters brought to light the ethical problem that forms the rottenest block in the foundation of big-time college football: amateurism. That is the spot through which he and his buddy Bloom crawled ratlike onto center stage.

Remember that the forty-three players who signed with Walters and Bloom were worshiped college stars from all over the country—from SMU, Pittsburgh, Clemson, Notre Dame, Auburn, Ohio State, Nebraska, Michigan, Iowa, Texas Tech, Illinois, Florida, Houston, Temple, and others—and not criminals or bench warmers or shirkers of their football duties. They were impact players, all-conference choices and all-Americans. Also remember that the attainment of money is not an evil thing in the United States, that learning how best to pursue a career in which one can earn a good living is one of the more important reasons one goes to college in the first place. And these players, who to all appearances were reaping the best of the rewards their sport has to offer in adulation and fame, had no hesitation in taking money from agents when their coaches and everyone else associated with the college sports programs told them they could not and should not.

There are three obvious reasons for this. One, the athletes had been performing something they were very skilled at before paying audiences for a long time without getting paid themselves for those performances, and they were tired of that. Two, they sensed that the rules they were urged to follow were hypocritical and designed for the benefit of somebody in power somewhere, but certainly not for them, the unpaid laborers. Or three, they had already grown cynical from watching their coaches and the system around them, had already taken whatever under-the-table money they could, and saw no reason not to line their pockets a little more.

Walters himself was very perceptive about the cynicism and immorality of the amateur system, though his arrogance tainted whatever truths he happened to stumble upon as he threw money left and right, buying players the way a trader buys parcels of wheat.

"I have done nothing wrong, illegal, or immoral," he crowed back in the spring of 1987 when he first hit the sports pages by suing six college players for breaking their contracts with him. "In fact, I've helped [more than one young man's] family and allowed him ten thousand, twelve thousand, fifteen thousand dollars, knowing he'll be worth a million dollars. Why not let the family have the niceties of life or in some cases the necessities? I've helped put tires on cars."

Of course, Walters didn't mind if he blew the car doors off the NCAA and its rule book in the process. "Let the NCAA fold. Give the schools the right to hire kids and put them on salary. All they are is farm teams for the NFL. Look what the schools do when a kid is in high school. They don't care then whether he's a student. Every school is offering them everything. I wasn't even a big fan of sports and I was aware of what was going on."

It doesn't take a big fan of sports to see what's going on these days, but sadly it often takes a criminal like Norby Walters to make us aware of basic abuses in our society. And amateurism is one of those. Not that there's anything new about the essential unfairness and phoniness of amateurism—the hypocrisy of the system has been there since the start—it's just that we like to forget about such distractions while we're enjoying the spectacle of, say, the Fiesta Bowl, with two well-marketed teams playing in prime time for the national championship. Because we crave college football for its entertainment value, we would, in truth, like to forget about everything that is wrong with the game.

But as far back as 1915, essayist William T. Foster was writing in *The Atlantic Monthly,* "Only childlike innocence or willful blindness need prevent American colleges from seeing that the rules which aim to maintain athletics on what is called an 'amateur' basis, by forbidding players to receive pay in money, are worse than useless because, while failing to prevent men from playing for pay, they breed deceit and hypocrisy." And more recently author Tom Wolfe, he of the white suits and gentrified civility (and certainly no athlete or sports buff), wrote, "If we train our athletes as mercenaries, they are going to conduct themselves in the highest spirit of the mercenary, which is loot, pillage and rape."

And that has happened. By denying big-time football players certain basic rights, we have turned them into grasping mercenaries with the most twisted of ethical backbones. And in recent years there has been enough raping, pillaging, and looting—not to mention drug-dealing, assaulting, and sporadic shooting—by college athletes to qualify some teams as invading armies and their coaches as Attila the Huns.

Forcing players to maintain the facade of amateurism is particularly vile considering the amount of money the NCAA and now the CFA (the College Football Association, bargaining arm for sixty-four big-time programs) generate at the players' expense. In 1988 alone, the 104 Division I-A football teams earned more than $500 million through gate, TV, and licensing receipts and supported thousands of coaches, athletic-department administrators, assistants, trainers, maintenance men, ticket sellers, and assorted leeches (there are usually a few old-time guys hanging around every athletic department under the ruse of being Vice-Associate Athletic Director for Community Locker-Room Affairs or the like) as well as most of the men's and women's sports teams at the schools.

Postseason bowl games have become monstrous moneymakers. Schools participating in the Gator Bowl take home $1 million; those in the Cotton Bowl $2.5 million; those in the Sugar or Orange Bowl $2.75 million; and the Big Ten and Pac Ten representatives in the Rose Bowl get $6 million each. And if that doesn't sound like a lot of money to you, because of inflation or whatever, wait until next year when the sum increases. True, members of conferences must split their booty with the other members, but independents such as Notre Dame, Miami, West Virginia, Florida State, and Syracuse get to keep it all. And some matchups, such as the 1989 contest between 11-0 Notre Dame and 11-0 West Virginia, are so attractive that bowl committees will get into unofficial bidding wars to entice the schools, like the one that drove the Fiesta Bowl's offer to Notre Dame up to $3 million. "We will do whatever it takes to get Notre Dame," said Fiesta Bowl spokesman Bill Shover. And what it takes is money.

Yes, money makes the world go around, even—especially?—in amateur sport. The sponsors for the Texas-Oklahoma game are soon to guarantee each school $1 million, and that's for a regular-season bout. I have covered that border war at the Cotton Bowl in Dallas, and after witnessing the great public parading and drinking and posturing and "Hook 'em Horns!" and "Boomer Sooner!" screaming all along Commerce Street for two nights before the game, I feel certain both states would implode from ennui and post–oil boom depression if the game were not played annually—at any price.

Remember, too, that the players see what is going on. They see the full stands. They see the TV cameras, the souvenirs, the rich alums, the cash registers. Even though they also need the game—as Pete Gent has stated of NFL players futilely grubbing for bigger paychecks, "Deep down we all know they'd do it for free"—they sense intuitively that something unjust is going on. I certainly did. I remember running into Ohio Stadium with my Northwestern University teammates to a deafening boo from 88,000 Ohio State fans and thinking that college football is so much bigger than the simple extracurricular activity people told me it was. The whole scene was very disconcerting: if my teammates and I were just amateurs, then why was this game such a big deal to so many paying adults?

With cash so much a part of the trappings of the sport, why shouldn't players feel entitled to a share? Philadelphia Eagles defensive end Reggie White, who has admitted accepting money while playing at the University of Tennessee, says the day will soon come when college players will simply strike for money. "Some of these athletes are going to get mad and they're going to walk," White says. "They're not going to play. They're going to finally realize what the NCAA is doing to them. Is it fair for the university to keep making millions and millions of dollars off a kid? Everybody says, 'Well, they're getting a scholarship.' That's true. But do you have enough money to wash your clothes, which they don't? Do you have money to go to the movies, which they don't?"

I doubt very much that a player strike will occur anytime soon, however justified it might be, simply because incoming college players are just kids who have been taught to respect adults and because nobody wants to jeopardize a budding career by making himself a martyr. But why can't we pay athletes? I mean, why? If a bowl game brings in $2 million to an athletic department, why can't the department give each of the top forty players, say, two grand as soon as the game check clears, and the fifty or so scrubs $1,500? What is wrong with that? Hell, reporters on the student newspapers earn hard, cold cash for their work—$500 a month at *The Daily* of the University of Washington, for instance. Are they more professional than athletes?

At Du Sable High School in Chicago's southside ghetto, a program called the Life Enrichment Program awards a new car to the graduating valedictorian each spring, as well as watches, calculators, or radios to the top ten students, and small gifts to anyone who graduates. Du Sable's dropout rate is 59 percent, and the program is a way to encourage students to graduate and to tell them "there is a way to break the cycle of poverty and the shameful dependence on aid from the government," according to its founder, the Reverend T. L. Barrett, the pastor of the Life Center Church near the school. Melanie Henry, who won the new Plymouth Horizon in 1987 by topping her class with a 3.7 grade point average, said that the auto sends a message to students that "they have to work really hard because a lot of good things are waiting for them senior year." That's right. A new car is a good thing, isn't it, a nice reward for hard work? Then how strange that it's pure evil if a college football player gets one for his hard work.

Amateurism is peculiar to sport, and that should tell us something about its validity right there. (Sport has long been overloaded with almost as much myth, hyperbole, downright fabrication, and psychological baggage as war.) If you asked a neighborhood kid to come to your house and rake your leaves, would you have the gall at the end of the day to say, "Thanks a lot, son. Hope the raking was a good experience for you. I'd love to pay you, but you're an amateur''? Does anyone think that money corrupts a child leaf-raker? On the contrary, the boy would be praised for his drive by all decent Americans and probably overpaid for his work.

Even the tooth fairy shows us as children that something as mundane as a growing pain, that lost eyetooth, can be rewarded and assuaged with cash. Why can't sport be seen in the same way?

Because sport is supposed to be its own reward.

The reasons for this perception are long and involved, but at its root is the assumption—basically correct—that playing sports is fun, that it is joyous liberation from the prison of the mind. As G. K. Chesterton wrote near the turn of the century in an essay on education, ''Earth is a taskgarden. Heaven is a playground.''

Well, sport is fun, but then so is painting. Picasso didn't give his paintings away, even the ones he made as a kid. When done with diligence, craft, and discipline, any endeavor, regardless of how much fun it may be for the doer, is also labor. ''World-class athletic performance, for the entertainment of millions of paying customers, is *work*,'' writes Leonard Koppett in *Sports Illusion, Sports Reality*. ''Work *should* be rewarded.'' People always say to me, ''Sure, you didn't get paid to play college ball, but you got to play in front of all those people. What about that?'' What about it? Frank Sinatra plays in front of a lot of people, but that didn't prevent him and Sammy Davis, Jr., and Liza Minnelli from demanding a million dollars a night during their recent tour of Japan. Something can be pleasurable to do—I've got to assume Ol' Blue Eyes still likes crooning—but your reward has nothing to do with that. At its purest level, a performance brings pleasure to its observers, and the observers honor the performer by paying him in some way. If applause is enough for the performer, fine. If self-fulfillment is enough, wonderful; we wouldn't have charity otherwise. But if the performer wants something more tangible—say dollar bills—then he can either get them or withhold his services.

But a college football player can't do this, because he has nowhere else to give his performance. Universities have a monopoly on high-level football for young men in their late teens and early twenties. And while exploitation and hypocrisy in any form is bad enough—and make no mistake, the nonpayment and subsequent abuse of socially powerless athletes is simply a form of modern-day slavery—the greatest evil is the way this hypocrisy has been institutionalized at our citadels of higher learning. Football players lie and cheat and make deals with snakes like Norby Walters and boosters because they see that's how the colleges want the game to be played. And generations of college students grow up observing this nonsense, seeing the double standard for athletes—the lowered entrance qualifications, the football dorms, the training facilities, the Mickey Mouse courses that keep jocks "eligible"—and they know that even in college the truth isn't honored.

"The sad thing is that universities are supposed to be crystalline pure," Alan Nicewander, the chairman of the psychology department at Oklahoma told me on one of my recent trips to the football cesspool at Bud Wilkinson Hall in Norman. "This is where you are supposed to learn about ethics."

But if amateurism is such a corrupt concept, why has it lasted so long in our colleges? Three reasons, says Leonard Koppett.

Because it is an exceptionally effective mechanism for the production of:

1. Cheap labor.
2. Positions of power and control that offer significant rewards to those who hold them.
3. An illusion of idealism that ranks among the best devices available for the illusion-making process that fuels spectator interest.

The first two points are easily understood: cheap labor comes from the unpaid players; positions of power and control are held by NCAA employees, coaches, athletic-department staffers, booster-club members, school presidents in their skyboxes, etc. But the third needs some explaining.

We are fascinated with the Olympic ideal, the belief that the way sport is supposedly performed in the Olympics, the way it has been performed throughout history—by amateur athletes performing for free for the sheer love of sport—is the way it should be done here and now on college campuses. But this rationale is riddled with holes, and you can drive a truck through any of them anytime you want. To begin with, the Olympics, which started eight hundred years before the birth of Christ and ended in 343 A.D. before being resumed in 1892, had *nothing* to do with amateurism. "Ancient amateurism is a myth," states classicist David Young in his perceptive work, *The Olympic Myth of Greek Amateur Athletics.* Ancient Olympic champions were rewarded with prizes of staggering value such as oxen, horses, vases of precious olive oil, tripods, property, pensions, and drachma. "The value of some awards would be in the hundreds of thousands of dollars today," said Olympics scholar Andrew Strenk. Nor was the ancient Olympic athlete shy about receiving those prizes.

"The whole concept of amateurism would have been incomprehensible to ancient Greeks," says Strenk. "You had to be a professional to compete in the Olympics, which meant that you had to prove you were a full-time athlete and that you had been doing nothing but training prior to the Games. The Greeks put tremendous emphasis on excellence, on having the best of everything. Modesty was not a big quality for them. They were similar to, well, modern-day yuppies."

So where did the glorification of false Olympic amateurism come from? From Victorian England, largely, which revised history to fit the social climate and class system of the late 1800s in Britain and much of Europe. With the advent of the Industrial Age and the surge in leisure time available to men of means—and increasingly to common laborers, too—sport took on new importance. Those who had the time and money to engage in friendly matches of tennis, croquet, archery, badminton, rowing, and the like certainly didn't want the yammering lower classes participating with them and sullying the grandeur of their lawns, lakes, clubs, and universities. So they embraced the concept of amateur sports, justifying it as an ancient Grecian ideal, and wielded it like a club against the proletariat.

In the 1870s the aristocratic British Amateur Rowing Association separated itself from the dirty-fingernail crowd by passing a rule stating that no person is an amateur "who is or ever has been by trade or employment for wages a mechanic, artisan, or labourer, or engaged in any menial duty." Obviously, only the very rich or terminally lazy need apply for club membership. Since the writing of that rowing law, states historian Ronald A. Smith in his seminal book, *Sports and Freedom: The Rise of Big-Time College Athletics,* "nearly every definition of an amateur in sports has been a negative one." Smith adds that "there appears never to have been a successful, positive, workable definition of amateurism, even as amateurism has served principally the social and economical elite since the mid-1800s." He then goes on to quote philosopher Paul Weiss, who wrote in *Sports: A Philosophic Inquiry,* "A rich man does not need to become a professional player. Since he has more leisure time than most, he also has more time to devote to sport. As a consequence, he may become an amateur athlete. . . . By and large the line between amateur and professional is mainly a line between the unpaid members of the privileged class and the paid members of an underprivileged class."

So what does all this mean? It means that amateurism is not really a moral issue about getting paid or not paid for athletic competition, but is a distinction by class. Amateurism ascribes a certain gentlemanly quality to itself—sport for sport's sake, rowers in neat white cotton suits toiling briefly, then reclining with crystals of champagne and caviar on lush greens while servants and ladies quietly come and go. What it has to do with is the notion of less proficiency than one might find in professionalism, of some vague feeling of innocence and wealth-induced optimism, of something that can only be described as the amateur *attitude*.

The trouble here is that making amateurism contingent on an attitude rather than a true state of being leads, as Smith observes, "to a dilemma of rather large proportions. First, external judges can never prove the motives, the state of mind or attitude, of the amateur. Second, the historic claiming of positive virtues of the amateur relative to the professional is a false concept. There is simply no evidence that an amateur is more virtuous than a professional. In fact, the reverse may be true, for the amateur at the upper levels of competition often received financial advantage for participation in amateur sport—certainly a hypocritical stance. This has been the situation in college sport since the 1880s."

Smith is a professor of sports history at Penn State, which, as we all know, has produced a few decent football teams in recent years. Smith and I had a nice conversation in the spring in which he said he felt that Nittany Lions' head coach Joe Paterno was doing about as good and ethical a job as a college coach could do, but that even Paterno, *Sports Illustrated*'s Sportsman of the Year in 1987, was stuck in the mire of hypocrisy—as are all big-time college coaches. "The hypocrisy of amateurism is tolerated because of the importance of football to society," Smith said. "Society wants it, maybe needs it."

I agreed with him that people wanted it this way, but I told him I thought getting the truth out could make the public re-evaluate its wants.

The good professor chuckled. "If you think you're going to change things," he said, "I doubt it."

Well, what the heck. Can't blame a guy for trying. As I said, when this book is done—win, lose, or draw—I'm out of here.

Just one more thing from Smith's writings, though, before we move on. To make it abundantly clear, as he says, to "those who believe that at one time American college athletics were purely amateur, a paragon of athletic amateur virtue," Smith offers this: "There are two problems with that belief. First, one must believe that amateur athletics equate with virtue; second, that they were once without a professional element. The first is debatable; the second is simply not true."

And how. Money and its corrupting influence (corrupting to people who believe in amateurism, that is) were there from the get-go. The very first intercollegiate contest in the United States, a crew race between Harvard and Yale held on Lake Winnipesaukee, New Hampshire, in 1852, was funded by the Boston, Concord, and Montreal Railroad, which saw the event entirely as a commercial venture. Both teams had all expenses paid by the railroad, and the winning Harvard team received an expensive set of matched black walnut oars for its performance. College track runners in the late 1800s routinely were awarded cash prizes; college teams rowed in regattas for purses of $500 cash and even for pure silver goblets—worth, according to journals of the time, double what an average laborer might earn in a year.

Other aspects of commercialization and professionalism were also there from the start: "tramp" athletes, sham students, boosters, etc. The very first intercollegiate football game ever played—Rutgers versus Princeton in 1869—featured at least one athlete, and probably three others, who could have been ruled academically ineligible. A powerhouse University of Michigan football team in the 1890s had seven players with no connection whatsoever to the university. And Fielding "Hurry Up" Yost, the famous Michigan football coach who once had ten live wolverines delivered from Alaska to Ann Arbor to inspire his boys, was himself the embodiment of the hired gun when he was an athlete. In 1896 he "transferred" from West Virginia University to Lafayette (Pa.) College just before Lafayette played the most important game in its history against the

University of Pennsylvania, which was riding the crest of a 36-game winning streak. With the 6′, 195-pound "freshman" Yost playing tackle, Lafayette won 6–4. Yost almost immediately transferred back to West Virginia, where he graduated a year later.

As has been said, nothing new under the sun. (Though doesn't it seem odd that a star football player, especially a tramp, might graduate?)

Why did our colleges adopt an indefensible system like amateurism in the first place? The answer has mostly to do with the social and philosophical climate in American society and American universities when the English model was first adopted.

In the early nineteenth century there were very few students in college—a freshman class at a big school like Yale, Harvard, or Princeton might have only 150 students in it—and since most of those students were from the upper crust of society, it made little difference if college sports rules were repressive toward those without money. Most importantly, college sports were started not by the faculty or administration but by the students themselves, and at the beginning there were no rules of any kind. The first American colleges were almost without exception schools with religious affiliations, run by clergy, and decidedly intolerant of pleasures of the flesh, including athletics. Students went nuts in this restrictive climate, often rioting, assaulting professors, burning down class buildings, and generally rebelling against what was known as "the college way." Unsanctioned sports were the students' greatest and least-destructive escape valve, and from the Revolutionary War until late in the 1800s students ran their contests pretty much without the assistance or blessing of the universities.

The school administrations got involved when they saw what a big deal college sport was becoming, and especially when they realized how much money sports could generate. Yale only seriously considered faculty control of athletics when it discovered in 1905 that its student-run athletic department had a reserve fund of a whopping $100,000 (about $2 million in today's money) and an annual income equal to one-eighth of the total gross income of the university.

Once they took over the previously renegade sports programs, university officials went heavy on the Olympic Ideal business as handed over from England because they could see that big-time, revenue-producing sport had no place in the collegiate world and therefore needed very careful justification even to exist on campus. The concept of amateurism gave the university brass this justification, as it still does today. No matter that the concept was taken from a staid, monarchical country with a strict class system based on pedigree and birthright and was foisted on a wild-and-woolly, adolescent, egalitarian nation where all men are supposedly judged only on merit (indeed, is there anything more democratic than the American field of play?), amateurism was just the lie that was needed. It was fine for the university to make money from sports, just as long as the students didn't. A more embarrassing institutionalization of hypocrisy is hard to imagine. As Koppett writes, "The lesson is inescapable: it is all right to do one thing while professing its opposite. It's not only all right, it is warmly endorsed and fostered by the leaders of society and all the authority figures who fashion a child's values. . . . In reality, there are millions of true amateurs playing sports everywhere—but not in front of ticket-buying audiences, for the purpose of mass entertainment. It's the deliberate confusion of two distinct functions—play and entertainment—that does the damage."

Certainly, amateurism would not be as offensive a concept if all students participated in sports, but they don't. They should, but they don't. Indeed, what is the point of college athletics if not to be used as a part of the total educational package for all students? Sports participation at one time was seen by many educators as an integral part of "the liberal education," but big-time sport today has nothing whatsoever to do with liberal education. At a large state university such as Ohio State or Minnesota, the football team makes up less than half a percent of the student body. The players aren't part of the college populace, they're unpaid workers imported for the entertainment delight of, by and large, TV viewers and fans.

The fact that there are no real rules for defining an amateur makes the power wielded by the universities and their mouthpiece, the NCAA, awesome. An amateur student-athlete is whatever the colleges say he is. This is a wonderful situation for the universities because they can wash their hands of any problems that arise from their inherently corrupt and immoral amateur sports system just by saying that whatever happened was against the rules. Whose rules? Their rules! A catch-22? No, this is something even better—catch-23, if you like. Yossarian had his problems with the circular insanity of the army, but everybody knows the army is wacko. But a college football player can't win because not only are the rules crazy, but the makers of the rules—American institutions of higher learning—have been traditionally seen as being ethically and financially pure as the driven snow.

Whenever a player gets caught accepting money or signing early with an agent or, God forbid, leaving school to join the NFL or another pro league before his eligibility is up, we react with instinctive horror. What a terrible and ungrateful human being that player must be! He has sinned against purity itself! But in fact, the "laws" he is breaking aren't laws at all, just whimsy. While it is clearly wrong for players to lie or break rules they say they will observe, it is also wrong to force them into lying or rules-breaking by making them work under an unfair system. After all, the universities could change their stance tomorrow—abolish the charade, pay their players, call the game what it really is: Age Group Professional Football, and become ethically sound institutions once again—but the players have no such options.

I sat in the Florida State weight room last fall with all-American cornerback Deion Sanders, and I asked him if he wanted to be in college.

"No," he said. "But I have to be."

Sanders, now with the Atlanta Falcons, is not the most sympathetic character. Weighted down with layers of gold chains and pendants (my favorite is a huge, dangling dollar sign that hangs just below the gilt words "Prime Time"), shades, and a vast amount of trash-talkin' jive, he seemed like Super Fly come to the campus. What was he doing at Florida State? He posed a genuine twofold problem: He was a reluctant, quasistudent at best—it would come out later that he barely attended a single class his entire senior year. And his presence on campus indicated to everyone—real students, fans, and critics alike—the extremes to which a university would go to produce a good football team.

Sometimes I wonder how some college presidents can look themselves in the mirror after seeing what mucked-up, hypocritical messes their football programs are. How can the presidents say they believe in integrity? What are they endorsing when they bend academic rules, fire coaches left and right, allow athletic directors free rein to wheel and deal, and simply bow down to their standing football armies? What are we supposed to think when we pick up the paper and see Bernard Sliger, the president of Deion Sanders's Florida State University, saying, "My general conclusion is that college student-athletes generally are not being exploited as many of us have feared. They clearly don't feel that way." Should I ask him if two plus two equals three? Should I laugh in his face?

Last November I read in *The Sporting News* a remarkable statement from a college president in response to an abysmal record produced by his head coach. The Miami (Ohio) University team was 0-7 through October 15 and clearly headed for the cellar. A reporter asked the school's president, Paul G. Pearson, if the job of head coach Tim Rose was in jeopardy. Pearson, according to *TSN,* bristled at the question. "The difference here, sir," he responded, "is that even though people are upset about losing—I'm upset about losing—we don't fire coaches because they lose. Our coaches know that so long as they do the best they can with the talent they have, that they have a clean program and that their young men and women learn to study and be students, they are O.K. We like winning. But a win without integrity is not a win."

I made a mental note to check up on Miami at the end of the season. Standing by a losing coach isn't so saintly a gesture, but it's an increasingly rare one for a president these days. It gets at the heart of the phony amateurism in big-time ball. If their college teams truly were amateur, presidents would hardly ever fire coaches. Why bother? But coaches come and go like bad stand-up comics, and presidents are always there handing them their walking papers. I wondered how naive Pearson was or how long he could hold out. Would he change his tune when the final won-lost numbers rolled in, or was he just as disgusted with the system as I?

In early December I looked up Miami's record, and sure enough, the team had finished winless, 0-10-1. At the end of January, I put in a call to President Pearson, just to see if his mood had changed since that *Sporting News* interview. I told him right off the bat I was writing a book on what is wrong with college football.

"That's going to be a big book," he chuckled.

He went on to tell me that he wasn't going to fire Rose, that in fact he couldn't do any firing anyway, even if it were to be done. The board of trustees held the real power, he said, and it trickled down to him, then the athletic director, then the coach. The president, he implied, was basically a pawn who could be ousted at any time by the board. There were nine members of the Miami board, all of them businesspeople, bankers, attorneys, and such, and they met five or six times a year and established policy for the school. "The problem in athletics rests first with the boards of the universities,'' he said. ''They wield all the power. At some schools if the president tries to turn things around, he's fired.''

Well, criminy, I asked, aren't presidents men of letters, don't they have ethical spines? Are they so gutless that they can't stand up to anybody?

Pearson may have laughed at my question, I couldn't tell.

''If you want to be the president at one of those big football institutions, particularly in a conference like the Southeast or the Big Eight or the Southwest—except Rice—you know you have to compromise your ethics. This is the perception in the business. You have a precedent at some of those places with trustees who hire presidents who will look the other way. That's the problem.

''Right here I've had alumni tell me I've got to reduce emphasis on high-quality academics because it's affecting the level of athletics. I find that incredible.''

It was my turn to chuckle. Hey, Dr. Pearson, I wanted to say, there are a lot of bozos in the world. Instead, I asked him to tell me a little more about this board.

All of them were successful in the business world, he said, and seven were Miami alums. All of them were appointed by the governor. One of the members was Wayne Embry, the former NBA center and now the general manager of the Cleveland Cavaliers. Wayne Embry. Hadn't I just been thinking about him? Why was that? It came back to me. Only a few nights ago Wayne Embry had been involved in a fight on the floor at a Cavs-Pistons game, along with some of the players. The NBA had fined him $1,000 for his part in the melee. Gee, that's an interesting kind of guy to have running your university. Wonder if he cares about won-lost records?

Were there any presidents who had taken the pipe recently for trying to slow down runaway football programs? I asked. Any guys with, ahem, balls?

''I know of one place, Oklahoma, where the president left not long ago,'' said Pearson. ''He tried to clean up Oklahoma sports and the board of trustees didn't like it. His was one of those 'resignations' you hear about. His name is Frank Horton."

Hmm, that rang a bell, but I couldn't quite place it. I'd written a lot about Oklahoma, but I'd never spoken with Horton. Where was he now?

"He left to be the president of the University of Toledo. He'll be there soon. The day after tomorrow, in fact."

I thanked Dr. Pearson and made a mental note to get ahold of Frank Horton one of these days.

A lot of people, even university officials, overvalue winning. I don't mean ethically; I mean financially. They think that successful football teams add great sums of money to their university coffers. In a later chapter I'll show that this isn't true, particularly with regard to alumni and outside donations to the school. But right now I'll point out how it isn't true even when considering the tremendous amounts of cash made directly by the team in the form of ticket, broadcast, and bowl-game revenue. All those millions of dollars go not to the universities' general funds, but to their athletic departments. And brother, is there a difference between the athletic departments and the schools.

It would bore you to hear how big-time athletic departments came to be set up apart from the general infrastructure of the colleges they serve. Suffice it to say that they have been set up that way and that the reason comes mostly from the fact that school athletics were begun by uppity students and from the start were excluded from the normal collegiate academic and administrative process. At most colleges the athletic-department administrators are not even housed in the same buildings with the rest of the school's officials, but are tucked in the friendly womb of the football stadium or basketball arena. Out of sight, out of mind, you could say.

At a surprising number of universities the athletic departments are not even run by employees of the school, but are handled by outside corporations. A corporation is a wonderful entity, we can all agree, a truly American device for the efficient exploitation of capitalism, but its goals would rarely seem to be the same as those of an institution of higher learning. Universities want to show a black bottom line, certainly, but corporations exist solely for that purpose. Clearly, putting an athletic department in the hands of a corporation is a risky venture, one that only further demonstrates the schizoid nature of big-time college football. Schools supposedly want to create intelligent, educated, ethical, well-rounded young adults. Athletic departments want to make a buck. Point. Period. Amen. And they do this best by winning, so, naturally, they want to win. They foam at the mouth to win. (Please note here that people don't follow big-time football per se; they follow big-time *winners*. Whenever somebody says, "God, I love Nebraska football," what they really mean is, "God, I love Nebraska's won-lost record.") And the school and all its rules and regulations about eligibility, class attendance, progress toward a degree, ethics, and the like stand squarely in the way of winning.

So what you've got are severe cross-purposes right there under one roof. (Or nearly under one roof, since the athletic department and the rest of the school don't exactly bed down together.) And that's a problem. That is hypocrisy. *Hypocrisy* comes from the Greek *hypokrisis,* meaning acting a part. Athletic departments act as though winning isn't everything. Universities act as though big-time sports is just part of the educational process.

In truth, athletic departments exist solely to promote themselves. Like flatworms, they have the genetic mandate to enlarge. And you thought when the football revenue poured in, it went to the general university fund? Hah! The athletic department uses it to buy more jocks and helmets. It uses it to pay for all the minor sports—the fencing, swimming, and wrestling teams. It uses it to throw parties and awards banquets, to finance recruiting, and to add more staff members, assistant coaches, secretaries, and Junior Vice-Athletic Directors in Charge of the Weight Room. It uses it to sing its praises in media guides and highlight films, to throw barbecues, to build Heisman campaigns, to recarpet the movie room, to build more and greater shrines to itself such as trophy rooms and greater and more ornate stadiums. It was, in fact, snobbish Yale University itself that built the first great collegiate stadium in 1914—the Yale Bowl (80,000 capacity)—thus setting an example for other athletic departments to build their own massive, revenue-producing arenas.

Those stadiums now are as much television studios as they are places to hold fans. And athletic directors are power brokers who work with television syndicators much the way network producers do: "Hey, Mortie, we've got a great package of live, three-hour adventure shows for your fall season! It's perfect—guys hitting each other, girls in little skirts, ad spots everywhere, and nobody knows the ending!"

The TV money rolls in to the athletic departments, and the athletic departments continue to complain about how overworked and underfunded they are. In a way, they are underfunded, but that's only because they spend whatever comes in and then increase their own budgets so that they can continue to, as athletic directors say, "stay competitive with the other schools." In other words, continue to win. It is a never-ending spiral, a worm that will eat anything that comes near it.

It is true that big-time football programs, with a little help from the big-time basketball teams, generate most of the money that keeps the minor sports afloat, with football typically providing 75 percent or more of the entire athletic-budget funds. But that in itself is crazy. If sports are of value at all to the university, they should no more have to support themselves than, say, the math department should. Making the football team pay its lesser brethren's way only justifies the athletic director's bleatings about how poor he is. It also provides the school with an excuse to turn the athletic department over to those aforementioned corporate types, who go right for the bottom line.

That's what officials did at the University of Illinois a few years ago, setting up a separate corporate entity called the Athletic Association to run Illini sports. Only last fall State of Illinois auditor general Robert Cronson recommended that the scandal-swamped AA be scrapped and the university take over direct control of its own athletic program. In December the school did just that, stunning a lot of folks who didn't know a university could relinquish control of its sports teams in the first place. Athletic Director Neale Stoner, who had resigned under pressure in July when it was discovered after a university investigation that he had, among other things, used athletic department funds for his own benefit, was furious that he came under criticism. He said the Athletic Association got a good return on its investment during his eight-year administration. He had been asked to make money for the school, and he had done that, he said. "They knew what they were after," he snapped. "And they got that. We were successful."

You have to be successful—make a buck—or else the athletic department is in trouble. Think what kind of pressure that puts on the athletes. I spoke with the athletic director at a large eastern independent school a couple of years ago, and he told me how in the last regular-season game the team's freshman wide receiver had dropped a critical, last-second pass and the team had lost, thus blowing a chance to appear in a premier postseason bowl game. If the player had made the catch, the team was in the big bowl game. It was that simple; the bid was conditional on a win.

"That poor kid cost us one million dollars," said the AD. "That's all there is to it. A teenager."

And do you think that teenager doesn't know it?

The University of Wisconsin athletic department has fallen on hard times recently because of declining attendance at football games. In the fall of 1987 the Badgers averaged 59,256 people for seven home games at 76,293-seat Camp Randall Stadium, the lowest average attendance in seventeen years. Last season they averaged under 50,000 per home game, mainly because the team was terrible, finishing with a 1-10 record after going 3-8 the previous season. The department is now a couple million dollars in the red, and the way for it to get out of the red, obviously, is to put a good football team out on the field. "The bottom line is that we have to be successful again," says Athletic Director Ade Sponberg.

That's a nice little burden for the players to lug around on their shoulders. "Hey, you dimwits," the AD is saying, "if you don't kick some tail on Saturday you're going to cause severe trauma to the athletic department, and the cross-country and gymnastics team may get the ax because of it."

It is at exactly this point—when the pressure is on the football program to produce wins—that corners start getting cut and the seeds are sown for rampant violations of NCAA rules. Watch out, Wisconsin, you may find yourself in the black but also on probation in the near future. I can't tell you how many athletic departments have followed that scenario: cut some corners, "buy" a good team, win a championship, get investigated, go on probation. Coaches and athletic directors will whine that this happens because whenever you win, you draw the NCAA's attention, and when the NCAA comes looking for violations, it always finds them because the rules themselves are so convoluted and vague that it is impossible for a school not to break some of them.

Hogwash. First, let me say that I also think the NCAA rules are ridiculous, but on entirely different grounds. I find them ludicrous because in their complexity all they do is further obscure a very obvious fact: Amateurism is a fraud and no amount of regulation can make it anything else. But the schools themselves become big phonies when they say they can't follow the NCAA guidelines. That's like John Adams and Alexander Hamilton saying they can't follow the Constitution and the Bill of Rights. Think about it. *They wrote the damn things themselves.*

It would be appropriate to say a word about winning right now, since, if we're not careful, that simple act itself—beating an opponent—may come to seem like a bad thing. It is not—not in college sport, not anywhere. Winning is wonderful. It is one of the main reasons we play games at all. Losing is okay, too—as long as you play to win. That is the key—not winning, but playing to win, giving your all, honoring your opponent by doing your best.

When coaches and players want to win—and they should want to—they will inevitably take advantage of any aspect of the game they can (hopefully, within the rules) to beat their foe. Competitors will always try to get an edge through practice techniques, coaching, scouting, and superior equipment. That's why games and athletic associations have rules, so competitors know how far they can go in their quest to win. But you cannot on the one hand reward only winners, and on the other hand expect athletes and coaches to behave as gentlemen, to play for the sake of playing the way someone who is "playing for free" should play. Amateurism has never worked here in America; by hook or by crook, Americans want to win. As Ronald Smith writes of the nascent intercollegiate game: "The spirit of winning quickly replaced any thought that participation in friendly competition was the principal end of college athletics."

If you make rules that state that all college football players must be students, too, the players (with the aid of coaches, ADs, and others who desperately want to win) will find ways to minimize their student roles and maximize their football roles, to get an advantage over their opponents. That is how it works. If you say the players can't receive money, somebody will slip them money. To get an advantage. The more rules given, and the more arbitrary those rules are, the easier it is for one side to get an advantage over the other by breaking them. Thus, the unethical and unenforceable amateur code guarantees an endless flood of transgressions—as long as winning is the main concern of the teams. Which it certainly is. Indeed, it is hard to imagine any sophisticated sporting competition in which winning isn't the main concern; anything less and you've got something like pro wrestling.

Still the NCAA refuses to face facts. It makes a proposal to add a twelfth game to the college schedule to raise more cash for the athletic departments at the same time that it takes away, for the first time in history, the prize money normally paid to college all-stars playing in the postseason Senior Bowl. No money beyond expenses, proclaims the NCAA, in a ruling too weird even to get agitated about.

At this year's Fiesta Bowl in Tempe, I ran into little Janet Evans, the 1988 Olympic swimming star, who was acting as the grand marshal for the Fiesta Bowl Parade. I told her I'd read in the paper that she was to receive $10,000 for her efforts from the planning committee. That's right, she said. But she couldn't take the money. Couldn't even put it in an escrow account or trust fund or anything. She was only a high school senior, and if she took the money, she would be a pro, she said, ineligible for a college scholarship and maybe even for NCAA competition. She giggled and walked off, and I thought, whew, I'm glad the NCAA is protecting us from people like Janet, evil little saboteurs consumed with greed.

Somehow, there are still many, many people who believe in the fabulous "Olympic Ideal," even though the Olympics themselves now are open to professional athletes in most sports. People still believe General Douglas MacArthur, former president of the American Olympic Committee, who stated, "The [Olympic] athletic code has come down to us from even before the age of chivalry and knighthood. It embraces the highest moral laws and will stand the test of any ethics or philosophies ever promulgated for the uplift of man. Its requirements are for the things that are right, and its restraints are for the things that are wrong." Too many journalists don't have a clue, either.

Last season John Eisenberg wrote in the *Baltimore Sun* that "paying the players is the wrong measure to take. It's a terrible idea." Players, the writer continued, "say they're being used, that they're generating millions without seeing any benefit. And that's sad. They just don't understand. They've been given a free education, a rare opportunity, one that offers their lives a foundation."

Ah, yes, the foundation. The education. That brings us neatly back to the Walters-Bloom trial, wherein Bloom's defense attorney, Dan Webb, decided not so much to defend his client as to attack the offended universities, arguing that it's hard to defraud institutions that are frauds themselves. Webb made college officials squirm on the stand by forcing them to recite the academic records of some of their star players. While at the University of Iowa former Hawkeye defensive back Devon Mitchell, who now plays for the Detroit Lions, took such courses as Karate, Ancient Athletics, Billiards, Tae Kwon Do, Introduction to Military Organization, Jogging, Recreational Leisure, Tennis, Advanced Bowling, and Advanced Slow-Pitch Softball. After the first semester of his second year, Mitchell, who would not graduate, received three F's, a D, and a C. After three years at Iowa, running back Ronnie Harmon, who also did not graduate and is now with the Buffalo Bills, had taken only one course toward his major, computer science. However, he had taken Billiards, Bowling, Soccer, History of Football, and Watercolor Painting, in which he received a D. Iowa also gives academic credit for participation in varsity sports, and Harmon was lucky enough to receive nine A's for playing football.

Linebacker George Swarn, a former Miami of Ohio player now with the Cleveland Browns, took college courses in basketball and racquetball to try to remain eligible. When he still couldn't meet eligibility requirements, he took an extension summer-school course entitled Trees and Shrubs. At Temple, Webb discovered, former all-American running back Paul Palmer flunked remedial reading four times, completed no classes in his major, and failed or withdrew from every course he took his senior year. Among the classes Palmer, who is now with the Kansas City Chiefs, did complete were Bowling, Racquetball, Human Sexuality, Adjusting to a University, and Leisure. Earlier at Temple, president Peter J. Liacouras had angrily stated he was going to strike Palmer's many football records from the school record book because the young man had taken money from Norby Walters before his amateur career was over. The president did not mention Palmer's academic record, however, apparently being satisfied with the young man's work in that area.

It is worth noting here that sports agent Mike Trope, whose first client was Heisman Trophy–winner Johnny Rodgers in 1973, had planned to testify at the Walters-Bloom trial but was not allowed to by Judge George Marovich for technical reasons. What Trope was going to say was that in 1984, when Bloom first became a sports agent, the vast majority of collegians selected in the first three rounds of the National Football League draft had agents before their eligibility expired and had taken loans in violation of NCAA rules. Trope wrote a book in 1987, called *Necessary Roughness,* in which he detailed the backroom dealings of agents and college stars. The colleges, he implied, know all about this stuff but turn a blind eye as long as the dealings don't get out and publicly embarrass them. That is precisely what con man Norby Walters and pal Bloom had done, embarrassed the colleges by showing the charade, and that was why they were going to prison.

In his book Trope justified what he and other agents did, writing, "I still don't think it's unethical for a college player to consult or sign with an agent before his last college game. I think it's okay if he does it as a junior; by then it's hardly too early to be thinking about a shot at the pros. An agent or a business manager or financial manager—at least a responsible one—is in business to protect a player's self-interest. To assume that it's wrong for a player to seek an adviser before his last college game is to assume that his interests are being looked out for by someone else, namely the school. That's a theory that colleges like to promote. It's a false theory.'' Trope notes that colleges do not provide workman's compensation insurance for the athletes, nor any kind of insurance against loss of future earnings due to injury, nor a share in the profits made by the college team. ''The rules of the NCAA are created artificially to protect the profit structure of college and pro football,'' Trope concludes. ''I consider the collegiate system one of the greatest forms of labor exploitation in America.''

Look here, I didn't set out to align myself with the dregs of the football world. I don't like sports agents any more than the next guy, I wouldn't trust Walters or Bloom with ten cents of my own money, and I know Trope has an ego as big as Donald Trump's. But these renegades, by slipping through the ethical holes in college football's regime, are the ones who make us confront our own hypocrisy. They may not be great human beings, but they know what's going on. Trope even relates this little tidbit, for those who think his era of agents invented corruption: ''In 1959, LSU's Billy Cannon won the Heisman trophy. Soon after, it was discovered that Cannon had signed a contract before the end of his senior season. Not simply an agency contract, but a pro football contract, with the general manager of the Los Angeles Rams. The general manager was Pete Rozelle.''

The people I argue with always say, ''But Rick, *you* didn't sign early with an agent. *You* got an education.''

True, I didn't have an agent, because I wasn't good enough. White cornerbacks who will end up as eighth-round NFL picks aren't exactly hot properties for men looking to make a living off commissions. And yes, I did get an education. But then, schoolwork always came easy for me, and I came well-prepared for college from an outstanding, crime-free, drug-free, clean, well-organized school district in downstate Illinois. My home was filled with books. My whole family read all the time. We had strict rules about how much TV we kids could watch. There was no going anywhere until our homework was done. In short, I had all kinds of advantages over a black, inner-city kid or an athlete with a learning disability or anybody who couldn't handle the unreal stress of trying to balance big-time football with the sudden responsibilities of the collegiate learning process.

But even though I got an education, I never really felt like a student. I was always a football player. I didn't have the time or freedom to do what other students did. Fall, winter, or spring, it didn't matter, there was always some football duty that took me away from the crowd. I regret that. I have always wished that I could go back to college and be a student who could take full advantage of all the things a university has to offer—the clubs, the intramurals, the discussion groups, the little things that happen while a football player is at practice or pumping iron or studying a wide receiver's moves. And today, even though a full ride to Northwestern has inflated to $18,000, at Alabama a football scholarship is worth just $6,500; at Colorado $6,800; at Arkansas $4,900. Minimum wage is $3.35; players at a lot of places would be better off getting a full-time gig at Wendy's to put themselves through school.

Believe me, that scholarship only heightens the player's sense of the hypocrisy. When my coach, Alex Agase, told me I'd received a free ride to Northwestern, I knew exactly what that made me: a pro. I was getting free tuition, room, books, and board at a Big Ten college. In other words, I was getting paid to play football. But I was an amateur. It didn't make sense. My parents took some of the money they had saved for my college education and immediately went on a vacation to California. Call it semantics, call it whatever you want, but a scholarship, when reduced to its simplest form, is nothing but money.

It is easy for universities to give scholarships to athletes instead of cash because they are dealing out assets that they already have in abundance. Dorms, bookstores, dining halls, classrooms, professors—what could be easier than sharing this operating material with a few more students? It is like a large fruit company paying its pickers with bushels of oranges gleaned from its own fields. It's money, to be sure, but it's cheap money. And it ignores a basic premise: What if the fruit picker hates oranges? What if all he wants is cash? What if the football player has no interest in an education? What if all he wants is cash? Sorry, buddy, this is how we pay: in books, lectures, and midterms.

When I played my first varsity college game in 1968, the cost of a year at Northwestern was approximately $3,000. That's what my services to the school were worth—$3,000 in the school's bartering system, if I would have paid that much to attend NU. While $3,000 isn't a lot of money, back then a good starting salary for a college grad was $9,000. Northwestern is a small, private school with inflated prices; I could have gone to the University of Illinois as an in-state resident on a football scholarship worth a little under $2,000. Of course, Illinois didn't want me at any price; they said I couldn't throw, which was true but unimportant for a high school quarterback who would soon become a cornerback—so we beat the Illini 48–0 my senior year as punishment—but that's another story. At any rate, what did I give Northwestern for its money? Here's how I break it down:

summer conditioning	80 hours
pre-fall camp	250 hours
regular-season practice	420 hours
winter conditioning	60 hours
spring practice	80 hours
film, playbook study, etc.	80 hours
Total	970 hours

A lot of this is speculative; you don't punch a time clock in college football. It's possible I have erred considerably on the downside. In pre-fall camp, for instance, we came to Northwestern three weeks before school started, worked out two or three times every day, stayed in a dorm by ourselves, obeyed a curfew, and were more or less captive around the clock. In my chart I only counted 12 hours a day devoted to football during pre-fall, but 24 hours might be more realistic. Then, too, coming to school early forced us to give up whatever summer jobs we might have had and lose that income as well. I didn't add in nearly as many hours as some players put in on weight-training. The heavy metal stuff was just coming into vogue when I started college; if you don't pump iron all the time now, you'll get trampled on the field. But back then some guys were devoted lifters and some hardly touched weights. I was pretty much middle-of-the-road myself, putting in maybe four hours a week on my own during the summer and then the mandatory team stuff.

I could have added more travel and hotel time. Even for home games players get on a bus Friday afternoon and travel to an off-campus hotel or motel to spend the night. And away games can easily take 36 hours of your weekend time. Sure, you're on a plane or a bus or lying on your hotel bed and you can study or read if you want. But you're not free, you're not a normal student. Just try concentrating on your medieval history paper while getting ready to play Southern Cal in the Los Angeles Coliseum. It's like reading the funny papers while parachuting out of a burning jet.

If you go to a postseason bowl game you can add an extra month of practice time, say, another 100 hours or so. And what about injuries? I haven't calculated all the time a player spends waiting in hospital X-ray rooms or going sleepless because of a pinched nerve or damaged joint or the like. The only way normal students get hurt as badly as football players is in car wrecks. And how about hobbling around campus with your leg in a cast? In the snow? With books in one hand? The minutes add up. My sophomore roommate spent most of one summer lying nauseated in bed while a ruptured kidney slowly healed itself. How many hours do you give that?

So taking the conservative number of hours—more than

twenty-four 40-hour workweeks—I was making about $3.10 an hour as an amateur in 1968, just about what I could make on a good night delivering pizzas for The Spot in Evanston, which I did. I'll get to that pizza job in a minute, but let's state the two main points first. One, when you play big-time college football, you're a pro, even though you're supposed to adhere to an amateur code. Two, you're a very poorly paid pro.

The hypocrisy of the whole arrangement is overwhelming. The rules are whatever the NCAA says they are. You can take what the school gives you, but that's it. You're not allowed to be given spending money, laundry money, movie money, or airfare home or anywhere else (except for school breaks and at the end of the year). And even more unbelievably, you're not allowed to have a paying job during the school year. So if your parents aren't wealthy, or if you couldn't save enough money from your summer job to sock some away—and remember that to be a good ballplayer you should spend most of your summer working out, not working—then you are an economic prisoner on a campus where there are most likely lots of rich kids with nice clothes and hot cars.

Which brings me back to the pizza job. For my last three years in school I delivered pizzas for a buck a pie plus tips for The Spot, a greasy little joint on Foster Street a few blocks from my dorm. This was in direct violation of NCAA guidelines. I did it because I wanted spending money, but mostly because I was hungry and I could eat all the food I wanted while I was working. (If you could only know the heartburn I experienced in college . . .) I knew that what I was doing was against NCAA rules, and I can tell you what that meant to me. Squat. Zip. Nada. The NCAA could take its rules and shove them up its big, bureaucratic butt; I was hungry. It was so clear how phony the rules were that any of us players would have broken any of the rules in a flash if it seemed like the right thing to do and the player figured he could get away with it. Such is the lesson of hypocrisy. I learned it. Mo Douglass learned it. Every college football player learns it.

Toward the end of my freshman year at Northwestern, a man walked into my dorm room and told me that I had won the James Lee Sterret Memorial Award for being an outstanding member of my class. Huh? I hadn't done much—just gotten decent grades and played football on the freshman team and pickup hoops at Patten Gym and had a few major drinking binges in Old Town with my pals and hitchhiked down to Indiana U. to see my older sister once or twice. And who in the world was James Lee Sterret? But a week or so later the man returned and gave me the award certificate and a check for $200. Shazam! What a great thing! Not the award, but the money. The certificate said I showed "promise of future usefulness," but how did anybody know that? The money, though, showed the right-now appreciation some real-world people apparently had for the way I had conducted myself as an eighteen-year-old student. The cash was going toward a trip to Colorado as soon as classes got out.

I remember thinking how curious—and how nice—to get university-approved cash for something as intangible as "promise," knowing that I could never get it for leading the freshman team in tackles or interceptions or anything else (which I didn't). Clearly, my football play—not bad, not great, but rather freshman-ically erratic—had figured somehow in the award-giving. But if I had taken the money for doing well on the university-approved football team, I would have been thrown out of school in shame and the James Lee Sterret committee members would have had to disassociate themselves from the athletic department for a long time.

I was thinking about this one day at the Multiplex while shooting around with Egypt Allen. The Egyptian and I started talking about college football, and he told me that while at TCU he was secretly paid about $1,500 a month and given a car to use. "I took a pay cut when I came to the Bears," he said with a wry grin.

I knew that he had been a prep all-American and one of the most highly recruited athletes in Texas history before he signed with TCU. I also knew that because of his money-taking he had been kicked out of school with six other star players and then been accepted into the Pre-Trial Diversion Program of the United States Probation Office, under which he would perform 250 hours of community service and pay back to TCU the scholarship money he had received on the basis of his false certification of eligibility. I also knew that he was a decent enough fellow, playing the game the way he thought it should be played, fast and loose. In Texas, he told me, it was understood by young athletes how much they were worth to certain Southwest Conference schools depending on how spectacular their high school careers had been. And he said most poor black athletes didn't feel it was wrong to take the money that boosters wanted to give.

I knew this was true. A little over a year ago I spent some time in Houston researching a long feature on Houston's Yates High School for *Sports Illustrated.* Yates is an inner-city school that in 1986 produced the first all-black team to win the Texas 4-A state high school football championship, crushing powerhouse Odessa Permian the way a steamroller crushes a pair of sunglasses. I watched the tape of that game, and my goodness, it was awesome. One afternoon I sat on the edge of the school's dusty, weed-covered field near the single, bent crossbar with a group of Yates players who talked about their football hopes and life dreams. Most of them said they wanted to follow football as far as it would take them, to play big-time college ball and then go on to the NFL, if possible. Some knew that they had already peaked as athletes and that they would have to scramble to milk whatever they could from the athletic skills they had. Some of the players came from solid families, but most came from broken homes and poverty; yet all of them seemed to have a fairly realistic outlook on their futures. Not blindly optimistic, but not crushingly cynical either. They all knew Yates players who had gone off and cashed in on the game—Reggie Phillips, Elvis Peacock, Dexter Manley. But they knew many more who had ended up in the streets, on drugs, in jail, dead.

We talked about money. The players all wanted it. Life was a hustle, the strong and the clever rose to the top. But that didn't mean the boys would resort to crime, to selling crack, or to violence to get there. These were high school athletes at a school where you had to make your own incentives, where failure was expected, where each day you had to ask yourself why you didn't just give in. These were the disciplined few, not the bad dudes. The boys told me how they would band together on hot Houston nights and scream at each other to keep one another from slipping into the gutter. Sometimes at the steaming summer-morning workouts they would cry from frustration. But they kept on.

Would they use the game? Would they take under-the-table money if it was offered?

They all nodded. Yes, they would.

Why?

"Don't you go to college to learn how to make money?" said one of the players.

"How could I sit down at a training table knowing my mom and sisters and brothers back home were going hungry?" said another.

I asked them if they despised the men at the NCAA for their repressive rules.

The players pondered this for a while. They were not mercenaries, not yet. They were just boys who loved football and wanted the good things in life.

"I just don't think those guys who make the rules know what it's like to be a kid," said one of the players after a while. "I don't think they even know who we are."

"Think about it," wrote columnist Tom Weir in *USA Today* recently. "Would any tuba player in the marching band not take a booster's handout? Could you have resisted it when you were nineteen?"

The larger question is, why should you have to?

I marvel that amateurism still exists, in the face of the case against it. Even a guy like John Cooper, the head coach at Ohio State and not exactly a freethinker, says, "It's time we gave these kids some money." But we don't like change, we humans. It upsets us. Amateurism gives us that coveted illusion that Leonard Koppett talks about, that sense that all the violence and money-spending you see out on the field is part of the innocence of youth, fun for fun's sake, my alma mater against yours—ah, the splendor and fabric and freedom from corruption of college life! I'm sorry, but it just isn't so.

Old Bo Schembechler, Mr. Michigan himself, testified in the Walters-Bloom trial that when he found out one of his best players, safety Garland Rivers, had taken money from Walters, he, Schembechler, chastised Rivers severely. "I told him he was a disgrace to Michigan football," said the coach. "His locker was closed and his picture was taken off the wall." So enraged was the coach that it seemed he would have marched Rivers to a wall, blindfolded him, and shot him if he could have. A man like Schembechler, schooled in mythology, doesn't have a clue.

I think now of Steve Young, the former Brigham Young quarterback currently with the San Francisco 49ers, who signed a gigantic contract in 1984 with the Los Angeles Express of the late United States Football League. The contract was for approximately $40 million over forty-three years, and while pondering it in a private jet carrying him back to his home in Provo, Utah, Young burst out crying. He cried all the way home, he said. He was simply overwhelmed by the sudden wealth and he worried that it would corrupt him. He came very close to giving most of the money back to the Express owner while keeping only a small portion to live on.

I ran into Young a year or so later on a practice field in Los Angeles, and I asked him what it was that had so unnerved him about his big contract. He said it was mostly the fear that his friends would look at him differently and that he might lose his sense of values, values he'd spent a lifetime developing. He wasn't as worried about that now. But he still wanted to show people that money in itself "isn't something evil."

Money certainly is not evil, Steve. But hypocrisy is.

STRETCHING

Because his birthday fell in early winter after school had let out for Christmas break and a lot of kids had gone on vacations or to their grandparents' homes, his mom let him have a half-birthday party in July as compensation.

The boys were dropped off by their parents, or if they lived in the neighborhood, they rode their bikes to his house. They wore old clothes, and after everybody had milled around the patio awhile they went out to the side yard and started playing football. That was the point. This was a football party.

One time they had been playing in his yard and one of the kids got mad about something in the middle of the game and stormed off to his bike and rode away. But today the boys mostly had a good time, even the ones who were slow and fat and had to block.

There were hazards in the yard, naturally, and they detracted somewhat from the continuity of the game. There were briars along one edge, a half-dead elm sapling near one goal, and a huge weeping willow almost in the middle of the yard. His dad had clipped the weeping willow's branches, but still they hung down low enough to whip your face like tentacles as you ran by. There was a neighbor's living-room window just beyond the bushes at the far goal line, but that was not a factor the way it was for baseball games—punting and kickoffs were strictly prohibited by his dad.

There was another field they sometimes played on at another boy's house. That was a long, soft stretch of grass flanked by a row of apple trees, and the boys loved to go there in the fall when the apples were ripe. But the boy's mother wasn't wild about the games because the players spent as much time eating her beloved apples as they did playing football. One time they sat in the trees and ate dozens of apples just after the trees had been sprayed. The mother was furious and said they all would get sick from the poison, but nobody did. It was typical adult hysteria.

Even though there were no fruit trees in his yard, and despite all the hazards, his yard was as good a place as any to play football. The games weren't brutal, because the boys were normal kids. Nobody forearmed anybody, nobody buried his head on a tackle. There were no rages boiling inside. And yet you could see already the traits that would be advantageous to the players as they grew older: speed, strength, soft hands, strong arms, cunning, intensity.

After several games they stopped and got sodas and walked into the woods at the edge of the yard. They sat at the top of a steep ravine that was connected to other ravines that ultimately led to the river several miles away. After a while one of the boys grabbed another and threw him down the hill. The boy tripped and rolled through the dirt and leaves and roots and finally stopped about thirty feet below the group. Nobody knew if the boy would cry or laugh. The boy growled and scrambled back up the ravine and grabbed the thrower by the knees, dragged him down the hill, and soon everybody joined in and they had a full-scale king-of-the-hill battle raging.

He got tossed down the hill several times himself, and after one heave he sat near the bottom, panting, with black dirt in his nose. The dirt was clean and smelled like church incense.

He made it to the top again and waited for bodies to fly by. Then he grabbed a boy and flung him down the hill. He stood up and for a moment he was the king. Then he saw the boys coming for him and he braced to hold his ground, realizing that this would be even better than standing alone on top, untouched.

CHAPTER 3

Your Coach Is the Greatest Teacher You'll Ever Have

To me, the coaching profession is one of the noblest and most far-reaching in building manhood. No man is too good to be the athletic coach for youth. Not to drink, not to gamble, not to smoke, not to swear . . . to be fair-minded . . . to deal justly . . . to be honest in thinking and square in dealing . . . not to bear personal malice or to harbor hatred against rivals . . . not to be swell-headed in victory or overalibi in defeat . . . to be the sportsman and gentleman at all times . . . these should be the ideals of the coach.

—Amos Alonzo Stagg

My college football coach was a block of a man named Alex Agase. He stood about 5′10″ and though he was paunchy when he coached at Northwestern, he weighed a rock-solid 215 pounds during his pro career, which he played for the Cleveland Browns shortly after World War II. He was a guard—I guess he went both ways, I think everybody did back in those days—and he was rough and tough as anybody you'd want to meet. All of the Northwestern players had heard stories about him from other coaches and old-timers who remembered Alex at the University of Illinois and then later at Purdue and in the NFL. He was a legendary competitor and a guy not to be messed with off the field. One of the more remarkable things about him was that he was the only Big Ten player ever to be named an all-American three times while at two different schools, a feat he accomplished by playing first for the Fighting Illini in 1942, then as a Marine trainee at Purdue in 1943, then going off to war and coming back and playing again for Illinois in 1946. While overseas he fought with the Marines on Okinawa and earned the Bronze Star and a Purple Heart. The best story I've heard about him comes from Joe Mooshil, a longtime sportswriter for the Associated Press, who was in the navy during World War II and who spent the months following the war transporting displaced Chinese and Japanese citizens between their two countries. ''I was on a train going from Taku Bay to Tientsin, the main city in northern China, with some other navy guys,'' says Mooshil. ''We were on liberty, and we'd been told to watch out for the Marines because they ran the train and the town. We were minding our own business and everything was quiet, when all of a sudden there was this noise as somebody tried to open the door from the other car. But the door was locked and the handle wouldn't turn. Next thing that happens, a huge fist comes right through the door, glass and everything, reaches around and unlocks the door. Scared us to death. In walks a Marine as wide as a mile. I get a look at his face, and, Jesus, it was Alex! I knew him from Chicago. We were old friends, and that pretty much guaranteed our safety.''

Occasionally we players would see Alex naked as he would go to the showers with the other coaches. No one would look directly at him if he was looking your way, but when he'd turn, you could see the old shrapnel wounds in his flesh.

Alex had a square head, jet-black hair, and an unlit cigar permanently attached to his lower lip. He was tactless, crude, single-minded, and in his way, fair. When he recruited me, he sat me down across from him at his desk, leaned back, chewed his cigar, and said, "We got some blue-chippers we're trying to sign. If they come through, we won't have a scholarship for you." Tactless, I felt, but fair. A couple of weeks went by and the blue-chippers must have signed somewhere else. Bingo, I had a scholarship and a college coach. Alex Agase was my boss, my leader. We had an uneasy alliance.

I like to think that in my sports career I was not a difficult person to coach. I was irreverent, prone to distraction, and easily bored, but I listened when my coaches talked and I played hard in games. After I had made the varsity, Agase would occasionally look at me oddly. "Telander," he'd say, "I want to talk to you later." Some days he would tell me things—about football, about how I could improve my game, about catching passes (I was a wide receiver before I moved to defense), about giving my all.

"It's in your mind," he said to me one day. I had been dropping more passes than I should have. "Woodring, get over here." Dana Woodring, one of our quarterbacks, ran up. He had a ball in his hand. "Stand there and throw to me," said Agase. "Hard."

The quarterback fired to the coach from ten yards away. Agase caught the ball. "Nothing to it," he said looking at me, the cigar nub at the corner of his mouth bouncing with his words. To Woodring he said, "Knock me down." The quarterback whistled the ball in. Agase caught it again. Woodring wasn't our best quarterback, but he had an arm, a gun, and he was scorching the ball now. If that football had hit you in the face from just thirty feet away—closer than any pass pattern we had—it would have caved your nose in like an eggshell. And here was old Ag, the guard with stubby guard's fingers, catching the ball again and again as though it were a slow-moving basketball. He caught ten passes that way. *Thunk*. Like nothing.

I was impressed and Agase knew it, but my pass-receiving

did not improve because of the demonstration, and the following spring I voluntarily moved to cornerback.

After I was a defensive starter Agase would sometimes talk to me about other things, serious things. He wanted to know about drugs on the team. "I've heard some players are smoking LSD," he said one day. I told him I didn't know anything about that—I sure as hell wasn't smoking acid—but that I didn't think it likely to be a problem on the squad. Those were difficult days for American society back when I played, 1967 to 1970, and it was clear the coach wanted to know what was going on with the younger generation. Or at least he wanted information that might relate to his team and his control of it.

One day tailback Mike Adamle and I went to the coach and asked if some team members could wear black arm-bands in the spring game to show our sympathy for the Kent State students who had recently been killed by National Guardsmen. Neither Mike nor I were campus radicals, but Mike's hometown was Kent, Ohio, home of Kent State, and I just thought it would be good to show our few spectators at the game that football players had consciences, too. Agase looked furious, but he grudgingly gave us an okay.

The next day he grabbed me before practice. "I didn't know you meant in the *game*," he roared. "Hell, no, you can't do anything in the game!"

To be honest, I understood his delayed reaction. Or at least I expected it, felt it was the only true response this man could give. Football was sacred to him. It meant a lot to us, too, but he was from a different era, almost another planet. He'd fought in the good war, almost died in it, and all this crap about Vietnam and jingoism and peace and love and protest and co-existence must have driven him nuts. Football and war were as simple as this: Kick the dogshit out of your opponent and the world falls into place.

During my last season it seemed to me that there were times when Alex looked baffled. It can never be pleasant to learn your land of black and white is really composed of shades of gray. And yet this was also his time of greatest triumph. We finished second in the Big Ten in 1970 with a 6-1 conference record, and in at least one national poll Agase was voted College Football Coach of the Year, his zenith as a coach. Indeed, he would have one more good season at Northwestern after that, and then his career would go rapidly downhill, first at Purdue where he moved in 1974, then at Eastern Michigan, where he was athletic director from 1977 to 1982 and where the football team went 0-26 at one stretch, the worst losing streak in the nation at the time, and there was talk of dropping the entire football program. I'd heard that the problems at Eastern Michigan had affected Agase's health.

For a time after I was finished playing, I didn't know how I felt about the man, about coaches in general. We won some games at Northwestern, but had I learned anything? Had a coach ever been good for me as a person, going all the way back to the start of my sporting career?

One day when I was back on campus for some reason or other, I ran into Alex. He looked at me and then reached around and grabbed me by the scruff of the neck. "Get a haircut," he growled. He was only partly smiling and he held on to my hair for what seemed like an eternity. My face turned red and a tidal wave of embarrassment washed over me. I was with friends who didn't know my coach, and maybe that was the reason for my uneasiness. There was something about the scene—the unexpectedness of his command (not that it was out of character for him, just that I didn't anticipate it in these surroundings); the unwitting rudeness of it; my sudden relapse into the subservient, sycophantic role of serf in front of the king, and his ready acceptance of that role—that absolutely enraged me. And yet all I did was chuckle and mumble that I'd be getting a trim soon. Which was a lie.

The scene has stuck with me through the years. I doubt that Agase remembers it at all—he probably did the same thing to dozens of his former athletes—but for me it captures the fraud of the big-time football coach as a teacher of young men. Put simply, a coach lives in a world that has little relationship to the real world, and his actions in his coach's world are performed to benefit or please him and him alone without regard to the feelings or development of those below him.

I don't mean to make too much of an adult's telling a younger person to get his hair cut. I've had long hair and short hair and just the other day my mom told me I looked like a wino with my current hairdo, but it is the imposition of one person's will on another person for arbitrary reasons that is always offensive. This is particularly so when the person in power attaches moral significance to his domination. When I played, short hair was good, long hair was bad. Why? The coaches said so. No other reason. They understood short hair because that's what they and their buddies had. That's the way they wore their hair when *they* played. It was right because they said so. I always wanted to show Agase the photo of my grandfather, Norbert Overstolz, posing with his football teammates back in St. Louis in 1917, all of the players with long hair and many with great mustaches. A player with a shaved head back then might have been kicked off the team for having a bad attitude. Fashion is always relative.

Big-time college football coaches like to profess that they are building proper, upstanding, freethinking, superior men at the same time they are building good football players, when that is clearly not the case. Far from socializing their players, coaches all too often shape them into young men with warped perspectives on obedience, morality, and competition who are often unable to function appropriately in the real world—that is, any world without football at its epicenter—until they learn new methods of behavior and thought. Writing in a recent edition of the *Journal of Physical Education, Recreation and Dance,* Professors James H. Frey and John D. Massengale of the University of Nevada–Las Vegas state that school sports and the teaching people associated closely with those sports—coaches, primarily—educate participants in a "dysfunctional manner." That is, the things players learn are not what they need to learn to be good human beings. "Selected actions, behaviors, and traits are often taught, reinforced, and then rewarded, although these actions do not reflect desirable social values," write the authors. "For example: How often is blind obedience taught under the guise of tenacity? How often is manipulation and deliberate rule violation taught as strategy? How often is composure and sportsmanship mistaken for lack of effort? . . . This list could go on forever."

I talked with a former Big Ten football player recently about how he was adapting to life away from the game for the first time in his adult life. He had been a successful linebacker in college, tried out for an NFL team, got injured, and spent part of the year on the team's reserve list before getting released. That was just over a year ago, and now he was trying to make a living in the real world. He shrugged and said things were kind of weird for him. "All those guys who were nothing on campus, the little guys I could throw out of my way, they're all walking off to their nice jobs," he said. "And I'm starting at the bottom. The stuff I learned in football doesn't apply."

Some of it does, of course—notions about trying hard and self-sacrifice and working toward a common goal with teammates are nice enough concepts—but much of the football rhetoric doled out by coaches is nothing but third-rate psychological pap sprinkled with clichés that have only the slightest basis in everyday life. Slogans that are useful in a primitive game like football—"Never surrender," "The most aggressive player wins," "Intimidation earns respect"—can be downright harmful in normal society where restraint, compromise, and cooperation are more typical ways of moving forward in the daily game. Certainly, some of the things coaches emphasize may help former players get ahead in some of the rougher corners of dog-eat-dog business endeavors, but nobody needs football to teach them those things. I have seen so many athletes who seem genuinely lost when their playing days are over that I would suggest that football does next to nothing to prepare players for the real world. There always seems to be a lag period during which a former player must put away the things he learned on the gridiron and begin adapting to reality. And while coaches love to cite their former players who have gone on to be big successes in various postfootball endeavors, those successes are often ones that came about *because* of the player's onfield success—distributorships and publicity positions and the like handed to the athletes for the players' marquee value.

Big-time football players also quite often have a very difficult time in their relationships with the opposite sex. In my years in locker rooms I have heard so much degrading talk of women by male athletes—particularly the use of women as objects to be conquered and dominated rather than as equals to be dealt with fairly—that I feel certain the macho attitudes promoted by coaches contribute (perhaps unwittingly) to athletes' problems in relating to women. In his watershed book *Out of Their League,* former Syracuse University and St. Louis Cardinal linebacker Dave Meggysey describes the sexual uncertainties of players that are exploited by coaches to promote fiercer play and greater obedience.

> [My Coach] got on me and began to chew me out at halftime. He said I was "afraid to stick my nose in there," as he always put it, adding that I looked "almost feminine" in making the tackle. This sort of attack on a player's manhood is a coach's doomsday weapon. And it almost always works, for the players have wrapped their identity in their masculinity, which is eternally precarious for it not only depends on not exhibiting fear of any kind on the playing field, but is also something that can be given and withdrawn by a coach at his pleasure. Most coaches . . . give their players a tantalizing hint of what it might be like to be a man, but always keep it just out of reach.

The increasing number of rapes and criminal assaults of women by football players seems to indicate that players can be poorly socialized or downright hostile toward women without being adversely affected on the field of play. The late James Baldwin wasn't speaking specifically of football players when he wrote the following about male sexual identity, but he could have been: "The American *ideal,* then, of sexuality appears to be rooted in the American ideal of masculinity. This ideal has created cowboys and Indians, good guys and bad guys, punks and studs, tough guys and softies [*football players and non-players*]. . . . It is an ideal so paralytically infantile that it is virtually forbidden—as an unpatriotic act—that an American boy evolve into the complexity of manhood."

I think of my Northwestern teammates, many of whom are successful lawyers, doctors, entrepreneurs, and executives, and I see how we could be used as proof that football makes good adult males. But I am just as certain that, for all our successes off the field, we are doing no better than any random group of Northwestern men from the same class. If anything, all we prove is that Northwestern kept up its entrance requirements for its football team and that we deserved to be in college. And then I think of some of the teams I have covered in recent years and of how many of the good players from those teams have had serious problems with society while playing football or soon after leaving school. Oklahoma has had so many players run afoul of the law that last winter one Oklahoma City newspaper toyed with the idea of running a Sooner All-Time All-Criminal Team, position by position.

It is important to remember here how soon the aforementioned "real world" is going to intrude upon college football players regardless of their skills; even if a player is lucky enough to make the NFL—and the odds of that happening are about one in fifty—the average career of a player in the big leagues is just over three years. All the things the coaches hammered into that player's brain will have to be expunged once he sets out on the street. Indeed, it is remarkable how many former players that I have talked to imply that *forgetting* about their coaches was one of the major steps they had to take to get on with their lives. They often still remember the coaches fondly or whimsically or even paternalistically, but those sentiments are merely the types of bonds you feel with anyone with whom you have been intimately involved.

To promote their own goals, coaches have become experts at brainwashing, at keeping their players up in the air, subservient, thankful for the simplest of rewards. I remember making a mistake on a coverage one day, and my secondary coach asked me what I was doing.

"When the flanker blocks down, I thought—" I started.

"Don't think!" yelled the coach. "Goddammit, *react*."

Not long after that I made a similar mistake, and the coach was equally incensed. I tried to make a lame excuse, but the coach interrupted me. "Why don't you *think* out there? Use your head for something other than a hat rack. Think!"

Coaches build you up to break you down; they break you down to build you up. It is a strange ritual of the profession, handed down, I assume, from latent boot-camp influences on the sport, as though the coaches are militaristic potters and the players mud. In *Instant Replay*, Jerry Kramer described Vince Lombardi's masterful use of the technique of contradictory rhetoric to put the Green Bay Packers players off balance and firmly under his thumb:

> Vince is letting up a little to get us ready for the Dallas exhibition, not driving us so hard on the field, but he's still riding us in meetings about being too nice, too polite. At the same time, he keeps telling us to play hard, clean football. The whole situation reminds me of *The Taming of the Shrew*. Petruchio beats on Kate to the point where he says something like, "See that beautiful woman," and she says, "Yes, that's a beautiful woman," and he

says, "No, that's an old man," and she says, "Yes, that's an old man," and he says, "No, that's a beautiful woman," and she goes along with whatever he says. Vince tells us to hate, and we say, "Yes, we hate," and then he tells us we have to play clean, and we say, "Yes, we'll play clean," and we accept everything, all the contradictions. Everything that Vince Lombardi says is so, is so.

How did it ever happen that we should hold coaches in such high esteem, anyway? A few months after Notre Dame won the national championship at the 1989 Fiesta Bowl, Volkswagen ran a five-page "special advertising section" inside the cover of *Time* featuring Irish coach Lou Holtz. In this ad Holtz wrote a thousand-word "Letter to the Next Generation," an essay that dealt not with football but the status of the American family and the proper way to raise children. "As I write this," Holtz stated, "I am thinking you will look back at our generation and refer to our times as the 'dark ages,' since the strength of a society is not found in the comforts of living but in its values, morals and concern for its fellow man." This from a man who, when asked what it felt like to be named head coach at Notre Dame, replied, "Look at me. I'm five foot ten, I weigh one hundred and fifty pounds, I talk with a lisp, I look like I have scurvy, I'm not very smart, I was a terrible football player, and I graduated 234th in a high school class of 278. What do you think it feels like to be named head coach at Notre Dame?" Holtz is an unusual man, a bright and cunning one, for all his protestations to the contrary, and he has much to say on many matters. But to have him lecture us on the state of American society?

Coaches acquired their ancillary roles as philosopher/oracles as a direct result of their swift assumption of responsibility for their college teams' successes following their introduction into the game in the late nineteenth century. "The introduction of the professional coach into college sport did as much as anything to accomplish the rationalization of intercollegiate athletics,'' writes Ronald Smith in *Sports and Freedom*. ''The pro coach began with the Yale crew in 1864, and by the early 1900s the coach's organization for victory was rather highly developed. The pro coach so dominated the athletic program among leading colleges that he was, at times, paid more than the highest salaried professor, and he was becoming as visible as the college president on the college campus.''

With this visibility came status, and with the status came credibility as something more than just a scribbler of *x*'s and *o*'s. People love the clear-cut certainty of victory; thus, they love winning coaches. Several decades after the Civil War there developed in America a growing belief that football could instill some of that now-romanticized Civil War combat manliness into an increasingly materialistic and effete class of university men. Football was ascribed all manner of masculine character-building powers as a peacetime substitute for battle readiness, not the least of which were the martial virtues of sacrifice, courage, and stoicism. Thus, the successful early coaches, men such as John Heisman, Hurry Up Yost, Pop Warner, and Knute Rockne, were seen not merely as victors but as triumphant generals, men who could keep out the invading hordes, protect us from evil, slaughter the Huns, and tell us about life as well. All of this was built on the premise that football was a glorious thing in and of itself (a notion the coaches certainly weren't eager to dispel), and that the coaches, riding atop this grand parade, had to be among the blessed just to be there. So, like hayseeds who suddenly find themselves being listened to at the city hall meeting, the coaches began to jabber for all they were worth.

We love our coaches because they are ''doers'' and because the games they preside over transcend our routine day-to-day experiences, and because it is comforting to think of them as being, like movie stars and lead guitarists, ''bigger than life.'' A few years ago I was down in Grambling, Louisiana, talking with ageless Eddie Robinson, the Grambling State University football coach for lo these past forty-eight years, and he was waxing eloquent about his own hero, Alabama's late Bear Bryant. It mattered not that Robinson had 305 career victories at the time, just 18 fewer than the Bear—and now he has 349, more wins than any other college football coach ever has or ever will have—he was in complete awe of the big man from Moro Bottoms, Arkansas. Never mind that Robinson was a black man coaching at an all-black school and that Bryant was no leader in the integration of southern sports (he once told Joe Namath he would never have a black player at Alabama as long as he could find a white one who could do the same job), his wins overshadowed all.

"He traveled over here to talk to the people one day," said Robinson. "And as we walked into the church where everyone was gathered, a little girl came up and said, 'Coach Bryant, is it true what they say about you?' The room was real quiet.

" 'What's that?' he said.

" 'That you can walk on water?'

"Coach Bryant thought for a minute. Then he said in that deep voice of his: 'Sometimes.' "

And that, Robinson implied, was what the folks wanted to hear. It was what *he* wanted to hear; Bryant was his link to the "real" college football world, the white one he and his teams had been excluded from for so long and in which Bryant loomed, Godlike. When Bryant died in 1983, the entire state of Alabama went into mourning. When Woody Hayes, already relieved of his head-coaching duties at Ohio State for slugging Clemson player Charlie Bauman, made a return to Ohio Stadium to dot the "i" in the OSU marching band's halftime "Ohio" formation, it was treated as though an archangel had descended to earth. The school later estimated it lost about $30,000 in halftime concession revenues because everybody in the crowd stayed in his seat to cheer Hayes.

True, times have changed since those last two men dominated the college football scene. There's less revival-tent fervor, but more video-conscious posturing. Coaches are slicker, more TV-aware and publicity-conscious than before, and far more interested in making a buck. Imagine a modern-day coach leaving after his death, as Hayes did, a bunch of uncashed, forgotten checks in a cluttered desk drawer. Or imagine a modern-day coach being so focused on football that he'd call up the player he had slugged, as Hayes did, not to apologize for the blow but simply to find out what defense the opposing team had been in. No, the guys nowadays would understand the damage to their image the incident had caused, and would be sure to make a public display of contrition.

But as I traveled the country these last few years watching coaches work with their teams, I got the feeling they would prefer things to be the way they used to be, simpler, more autocratic, less public, less commercial; that the money and recognition they now get is slim compensation for the loss of their absolute reign. In truth, though, as much as things have changed for coaches, even more has stayed the same. In 1905 Harvard paid coach Bill Reid the princely sum of $7,000, nearly double the salary of the average professor at the school, 30 percent more than the highest-paid professor, and almost as much as Harvard's president of thirty-six years, Charles Eliot. Except for the extra excesses of TV and radio shows, shoe deals, and the like, that is much the same coach-to-educator salary ratio as of today. Overcompensation didn't begin with Jackie Sherrill.

Look back at Stagg's list of coaching virtues at the beginning of this chapter. It is laughable in its innocence. I think of the drinking of Clemson's Frank Howard, the horse-playing of Earle Bruce, the smoking of Bear Bryant and Joe Morrison (who chain-smoked Marlboros right up until his heart attack last winter), the profanity of Frank Kush, the greed of Sherrill, the personal malice I myself felt emanating from Woody Hayes as I stood on the field as an enemy cornerback at Ohio Stadium, the double-dealing of Dennis Erickson, the current University of

Miami coach who said two days before he took the Hurricanes' job last March, "I'm staying at Washington State"; the ungentlemanly ways of so many coaches that I wouldn't know where to start.

And now with the influx of the black athletes into college football, the coaches, who are almost without exception white, are also failing a minority group that desperately needs guidance and role models. Blacks, virtually shut out of big-time college sports until the late sixties—I still find it hard to believe that my 1967 recruiting class at Northwestern had not one black player in it—now comprise almost 40 percent of the Division I football players and a much higher percentage of the sport's stars. The extent to which blacks dominate the upper echelons of football can be highlighted very quickly with all-star statistics. Since 1974, thirteen of the fifteen Heisman Trophy winners have been black. The 1987 *Sporting News* all-American team featured eighteen blacks out of twenty-eight players. The 1988 squad had fifteen blacks out of twenty-eight players. The percentage carries over to the NFL, where this year's *Sporting News* all-pro team featured seventeen blacks and nine whites. Ditto for the rising stars: the 1988 *USA Today* High School all-American team was made up of seventeen blacks, six whites, and a Polynesian.

The special problems of blacks on university campuses are things that football coaches are poorly equipped to deal with. Coaches are looking to manipulate and win, while blacks are often looking for identity. Buffeted by the demands of their sport, an academic curriculum they may be ill-prepared for, and the alienating, even hostile, atmosphere of white-dominated campuses—example: blacks make up the majority of the University of Oklahoma football team, but only 4 percent of the school enrollment—black football players are trapped in a pressure-packed foreign land. Indeed, according to a 1987 NCAA study, enrollment of black undergraduates at all 291 Division I football and basketball schools is the same as Oklahoma's, 4 percent. Add to the isolation the fact that many black athletes come from single-parent homes where there is no strong father image, and it becomes clear the power their coaches—their football father figures—can have over them. In a syndicated newspaper column entitled "The Disappearing Black Male on Our College Campuses," William Raspberry noted how difficult it is for young black men to organize cohesive, confident selves out of the conflicting, disorganized pieces of machismo and failure they see about them. "The crying need," wrote Raspberry, "is to find ways of playing to the strengths of black males without 'wimpifying' them. Our failure to do so may be one reason so many black boys disdain as 'white' or 'sissified' attributes associated with academic and professional success."

Part of the problem is that coaching, by and large, is a grueling, petty job filled with less-than-stimulating routine punctuated by sporadic, emotional binges—the big games. Most of the men who get into football coaching are men who played the game itself and are loath to leave its comforting familiarity or who can think of nothing else to do. As a group, college football coaches are not brilliant or even reflective men. But they are almost all cunning, clever, savvy, hardworking, dedicated, practical, and to varying degrees, sincere. College coaches have to recruit as well as coach, and so there are some who shine at that special talent. Penn State's Joe Paterno and Michigan's Bo Schembechler are masters at selling the long-time stability of their schools' programs. USC's Smith and UCLA's Terry Donahue promote the tradition and location of their universities. Switzer was always a wizard when it came to sweet-talking black kids and their mothers from the Southwest. Before he left to take the head job with the Dallas Cowboys, Miami's Jimmy Johnson was Switzer's equal in the Southeast. And some coaches, like Nebraska's Osborne, are so bland that they must win recruits simply by being who they are, the stewards of great football traditions at big-time universities.

Osborne, to his credit, is a bright man with a doctorate in educational psychology. But high intelligence can burden a coach the way a fine sense of smell can burden a sewer worker. A friend of mine, a former basketball player for Bobby Knight at Indiana, feels that intelligence is a large part of Knight's problems. Knight seems to come apart when the game of basketball does not live up to his high expectations of it. "I think Bobby is a type of genius," says the ex-player. "He's way too smart for the game." He may well be, but he's a dunce when it comes to personal relations. Still, Knight is light-years ahead of former Green Bay coach Vince Lombardi, another smart man who knew he was smart and who treated his players like animals, as though winning games could justify almost any behavior toward those beasts. In the book *Vince: A Personal Biography,* author Michael O'Brien describes Lombardi's tantrums over imperfections in his team's play that "bordered on maniacal egotism." During winning streaks Lombardi rejoiced over his success, but taunted his players: "Don't think you're responsible for all this success. Don't let it go to your heads and become impressed with yourselves, because I want you to understand that *I* did this. I made you guys what you are."

Vince Lombardi has done more to corrupt the profession of football coaching than any man before or since. Because he won games, and because he bullied his players in a way that quite literally dehumanized them, he opened the door for all kinds of abuses in the name of winning. I have had several Lombardi-type coaches in my own sporting career, and not just in football, and I strongly believe they did more damage to me and my teammates than they had any right to. It is very easy to be a Lombardi clone (although hard to win as frequently as Vince did, since he was a master of his own techniques, plus he had more talent than most teams as well as a draft to keep his squad refreshed), and that is because nothing is easier or more primitive than bullying and raging and demanding what *you* want. That is what babies do. That type of coaching may work, but at a great psychic cost to the players, particularly when those players are not twenty-five- and thirty-year-old professionals, but impressionable college-age boys.

I think it might be appropriate here to bring up the teachings of an expert on the psychological development of children, Dr. Bruno Bettelheim. True, we are not discussing children in this book, but in a way college football players are the children of their coaches, in the sense that the coaches have real and important control over the players, and the players crave the respect and love of their coaches and will do almost anything to get it.

In a provocative 1985 essay entitled "Punishment versus Discipline," Bettelheim explained that punishment and discipline are not the same thing, though many people mistakenly believe they are. Discipline is a gift of love, while punishment is the sting of selfishness. Bettelheim advises parents to heed Shakespeare's words: "They that have power to hurt and will do none . . . They rightly do inherit heaven's graces." The point is not, Bettelheim notes, that teaching correct behavior to a child (or good performance to a player) means that there will never be pain involved, only that such pain should arise from the child's own sense of wrongdoing and his falling from grace with his parent and the adult world in general, and not from the parent's annoyance, arrogance, or cruelty. At South Carolina a couple of years ago there was a defensive coordinator named Tom Gadd, whose nickname on the team was "Little Hitler." He was a small man with a mustache who pushed the players so hard in drills, made them run so much in the sweltering Dixie heat that they often dropped right on the field from heat exhaustion and muscle cramps. "He was brutal," says former Gamecock nose tackle Tommy Chaikin. "He made us run drills like this one called 'Escape from Saigon,' where three blockers would beat up on a single defender. And then we'd have what he called 'Packer Day,' where he could act like Lombardi and make us do up-downs until we couldn't move. It did nothing for us except break us down, physically and mentally.'' Punishing players ''Lombardi-style'' is such a common practice in college football that I have to believe that many coaches envy the man's legend so much that they think simply by adopting his ''style,'' they, too, will become legends. I lived for a while in Key West, Florida, and was amazed while there to see the number of would-be writers who likewise adopted the drinking, partying, and sporting habits of former-resident Ernest Hemingway, even down to wearing beards and Cuban shirts and talking endlessly about marlin, as though those things alone could win them a Nobel Prize.

Bettelheim's message about punishment is clear: If severe enough, punishment can sometimes bring about the desired actions of the punished, but it quite often produces the opposite of the desired effect and almost always leaves lasting marks that hinder ''the development of morality—that is, the creation of conditions that not only allow but strongly induce a child to wish to be a moral, disciplined person.'' In other words, it corrupts.

What's the point here? you say. Bettelheim was talking about children and parents, and we're talking about football players and coaches. But the similarity between the two groups is astonishing, even down to a football player's sharing of intimate personal problems with his father-figure coach. In a study of college players published in *Psychology Today,* Jack Nation and Arnold LeUnes, professors of psychology at Texas A&M University, noted that ''football players believed much more strongly than the rest of the students that other people had considerable control over their lives,'' and that the players ''placed great stock in the advice given by the coaches. . . . In times of personal crisis, a strong safety looked to the defensive backfield coach for reassurance and emotional support, a halfback to the offensive-back coach, and so on.'' Just read the following axioms from Bettelheim, substituting *player* for *child* and *coach* for *parent,* and you can see the folly of the tyrannical approach in forming good players and more importantly, good people:

''Punishment teaches a child that those who have power can force others to do their will. And when the child is old enough and able, he will try to use such force himself. . . .''

''Any punishment sets us against the person who inflicts it on us.''

''The more hurtful the punishment, the more devious the child will become.''

''Punishment is a traumatic experience not only in itself but also because it disappoints the child's wish to believe in the benevolence of the parent, on which his sense of security rests.''

So much of what coaches do to their players is done in the name of ''discipline,'' as though the pursuit of that virtue justifies almost anything. ''You gotta have discipline to play this game,'' the coaches say over and over. And it is true that discipline—the control of one's behavior to facilitate efficiency—is important for success in football, but no more so than it is in almost any other endeavor. And yet this vague thing, ''discipline,'' hangs over every football field, sought after like the Grail, but always slipping through the fingers, just out of reach. And that is because what coaches really want is not discipline but subservience. Running ladder drills until you stagger drunkenly for each extra foot may teach you that you can go beyond what you thought your limits were, but it also teaches you that the coach who ordered the drills is a tyrant. He justifies this in the name of discipline; the players see it as perversity.

Some coaches develop an almost casual cruelty as the essence of their style. I was eating lunch recently at a Chicago diner owned by Tom Runkle, a friend of mine from high school days. He was standing and I was sitting, and I noticed the little finger on his left hand. It was grotesquely swollen and bent. I knew he had played football at Arizona State in the late sixties under its brutal former coach Frank Kush, and I asked him if this ugly pinky of his was a memento from those days. He laughed. "Yeah," he said. "I was playing defensive end in a spring scrimmage and I caught the finger on a guy's facemask. I came out and Kush looked at the finger and said, 'It's just dislocated,' and he grabbed it and yanked it and when he was done, the bone was almost coming through the skin. He said, 'Tape it up,' and I did and went back in the game. That summer a doctor looked at the finger and said it was still broken, but the bones never grew back together and there was nothing he could do. It's useless now," Runkle shook his head. "Kush never believed anybody was hurt."

I think about the coach I had in high school, before I made the varsity. He wasn't a bad man—in fact, I liked him—but one day our first team sophomore quarterback had to go to the bathroom and he asked the coach if he could run to the locker room to relieve himself. The coach said no. The quarterback said he had to go, he had to have a bowel movement. The coach said no, that if he left the field he would be kicked off the team. The quarterback said he was leaving anyway, and he did. The coach drifted into his Lombardi mode, his tough guy mode, and that was it. The quarterback never played again.

Coaches give out so much contradictory information that a player who absorbs it all will find himself frozen with indecision, able only to follow the latest command of the coach, whatever it may be. I think of all the times my teammates and I were told to play with "reckless abandon" and then a moment later to be "under control." We were told to "have fun out there" and to "get serious," to "knock their heads off" and to be "gentlemen." At any rate, coaches who are out of control themselves cannot very well teach those under them how to be disciplined. "The original definition of the word 'discipline' refers to an instruction to be imparted to disciples," writes Bettelheim. "When one thinks about this definition, it becomes clear that one cannot impart anything, whether discipline or knowledge, that one does not possess oneself. Also it is obvious that acquiring discipline and being a disciple are intimately related.''

Do as I say, not as I do, has never been a good teaching motto. Players see their coaches berate referees, lie to the press, abuse basic rules of the game, chastise poor players, make exceptions for star players, and, of course, leave whenever there is a better job somewhere else, and they process this and, subliminally at least, realize that all the little things being taught them are fraudulent; winning is all that matters. I think about the former players from Wisconsin–Stevens Point, the ones who tied for the NAIA national title in 1987 and then had their crown stripped after it was discovered the team had two transfer players who were ineligible. In the wake of that scandal head coach D. J. LeRoy was fired, and one of those ineligible players, Keith Majors, hung himself in an unsuccessful suicide attempt in a county jail. LeRoy sued the school for unfairly releasing him and last spring settled out of court, with the school paying him $40,000 and acknowledging that he was not at fault for the players' being ineligible. Swell. The law is one thing, but if the head coach isn't responsible for having outlaws on the team, good God, who is?

''Character comes from above,'' says Joyce Alexander, a psychologist at Cleveland State University who works with that school's athletes and is a consultant for athletes from other universities. ''How can you expect players to show it when there isn't any demonstrated to them?''

How, indeed. And there is a real societal cost paid for coaches who try to break their players and control their behavior through strict rules and regulations and their thoughts through propaganda. ''To be disciplined requires self-control,'' writes Bettelheim. ''To be controlled by others and to accept living by their rules or orders makes it superfluous to control oneself. When the more important aspects of a child's actions and behavior are controlled by, say, his parents or teachers, he will see no need to learn to control himself; others do it for him.'' But they won't forever. Suddenly the player is out of school, on his own, and completely baffled. I have seen so many football players who struggle with the basics of day-to-day living once they are out from under their coaches' wings, who have trouble renting apartments, showing up for work on time, placing long-distance calls, simply doing things on their own—because they always have had someone to guide them along.

But the coaches aren't really concerned about the long-range effects of their teachings, because the coaches are rooted in the here and now. They know they are far better off winning with antisocial people than losing with well-adjusted ones. Again, the hypocritical messages sent down from the college administrations say one thing but mean another, and the coaches pick up on this and act accordingly. Temple University head coach Bruce Arians was fired at the end of last season after compiling a 27-39 record in six years at a school without a clear commitment to big-time football, but which nevertheless played such opponents as Pitt and Penn State. Athletic director Charlie Theokas admitted that Temple didn't have ''great facilities'' or lots of money, but said it was time to ''resell, remarket, reorganize.'' What he meant was embodied nicely in Arians's farewell statement: ''I got fired because I didn't win enough games.''

Also after last season, Stanford athletic director Andy Geiger stated it would be ''stupid'' even to consider firing head coach Jack Elway, whose 25-29-1 record in five years at an ''egghead'' school had to be considered at least respectable. A month later Elway was canned. College coaches have less security than anyone else on campus. They have no tenure and no union. Imagine, if you can, the chairman of the university math department getting fired after having a ''bad year.'' Just what is a ''bad year'' at a university, anyway? ''You know what they call the guy who finished last in medical school?'' asks basketball coach Abe Lemons. ''Doctor.''

At Alabama last season the fans got riled up when the Crimson Tide lost to Mississippi. Somebody hurled a rock through head coach Bill Curry's office window, and people began picking up the cry they had begun the previous season: off with Curry's head. The university president then gave the coach this ringing endorsement: "Any condemnation of Curry is premature." At the time, Curry's record at Alabama was 3–1 for the season, 10-6 in his two years there, and the team was on its way to an 8-3 season and a win over Army in the Sun Bowl. But the demand for wins never lessens; last week means nothing, this Saturday is all. The coaches are little more than Sisyphuses with whistles around their necks, endlessly pushing boulders up hills only to see them roll down again. As Pittsburgh Steeler coach Chuck Noll says, "A life of frustration is inevitable for any coach whose main enjoyment is winning."

Knowing that winning cannot be guaranteed, and that their job security rests on winning, coaches are forced to look elsewhere than the scoreboard for enjoyment. More and more they find it in the bottom line. When Texas A&M head coach Jackie Sherrill resigned last winter under a cloud of controversy, following a *Dallas Morning News* report that Sherrill had allegedly paid a player $4,400 to keep quiet about NCAA rules violations, his contract, which was bought out by the university, became a handy gauge for other coaches to use in determining how they themselves were doing in the salary derby. Sherrill's contract was not the best in the game, but it was not the worst, either, and it provides a glimpse at how lucrative the coaching business has become—and thus how much winning at any cost is rewarded.

Under the terms of the termination deal he signed in December, Sherrill immediately received $684,000 from A&M, slightly more than the amount he would have made in two years from his salary as athletic director and head coach and from *The Jackie Sherrill Show* on television. His contract had called for an automatic salary increase of at least 10 percent annually, or the percentage increase of the average faculty salary, whichever was greater. Sherrill also received a month's base pay for each bowl appearance "in order to compensate for the extra time needed to prepare for the appearance and for the tangible benefit derived [by Texas A&M] from such appearance." (Isn't it interesting that the players are supposed to put in that same extra time simply for the honor of playing in the game?)

The university also provided Sherrill with a car and required him to be a member of Briarcrest Country Club in nearby Bryan—at university expense—so that he could "maintain good alumni relations, vigorously recruit student athletes [and] esteem himself socially and morally." He also was allowed to "engage in speaking activities and charitable endeavors," traveling at athletic-department expense. In an agreement not mentioned in the contract, the school provided a five-year $150,000 loan to Sherrill for the purchase of his College Station home. Twenty percent of the loan was written off by the school for each year Sherrill was employed at Texas A&M. At the end of the loan in 1987, a second $150,000 loan was taken out by Texas A&M under the same arrangement. Sherrill had worked almost two years of the second loan, and the remaining $90,000 on the loan was forgiven by the school as part of the termination agreement.

Because Sherrill was expected to entertain alumni and recruit some studs, and because he might have to use his home for such purposes, Texas A&M paid the utilities and insurance on his $300,000 home. Sherrill was allowed to engage in outside business endeavors, but he was prohibited from engaging in activities that involved "the sale or endorsement of alcoholic beverages or pornographic materials . . ." although his business interests could include restaurants that sold beer. He was also prohibited from endorsing candidates for public office, a provision he appeared to violate the day before the 1988 presidential election when he appeared at a campaign rally featuring George W. Bush, son of then-candidate George Bush. Sherrill posed for pictures with Texas A&M "12th Man" T-shirts that carried Vice President Bush's name on them.

Two months before Sherrill's resignation under pressure, the NCAA put Texas A&M on probation for two years for numerous rules violations. As punishment the school was barred from appearing in a postseason bowl game following the 1988 season and lost up to five football scholarships for the 1989 season. There were a number of other sanctions imposed as well, but ironically, under the terms of Sherrill's contract, the sanctions were not enough to get him fired. He left, basically, because the university was spending so much time responding to the charges that it was unable to go about its regular business.

A school will put up with a lot of embarrassing behavior from its football coach as long as his performance doesn't get too public and make the university look like a total clown show. Woody Hayes, God rest his soul, was a buffoon par excellence who generally was able to keep his lunatic antics out of media range—otherwise he would have been canned much sooner than he was, even at Ohio State. Former quarterback Ron Maciejowski recalls the first time he saw a Woody tirade in practice: "First he took his cap off and he tried to tear it, but couldn't because it hadn't been precut. Then he took his watch off and smashed it on the ground, then took his glasses off and smashed them into the ground. Then he took his shirt off and ripped it right down the front, and he tried to tear the whistle cord which was hanging around his neck but couldn't, because it was too tough. So he got frustrated and punched himself in the eyes."

When I was briefly with the Kansas City Chiefs in 1971, I spent some time talking with rookie teammate Bruce Jankowski, who had played wide receiver at Ohio State, and I vividly recall him telling me how Hayes would beat on his own forehead with his fists, with rings on his fingers, until blood would stream down his face. Woody was always smashing film projectors, said Jankowski, and one time, when two stadium doors were locked with a chain, Hayes drove a tractor through the doors like Ben Hur parting the Romans. These are the kinds of things a college football coach can do, if he wins.

And make no mistake about it: Winning forgives all, no matter how embarrassing the situation. This point was driven home forcefully last March, when I found myself on ABC's *Nightline* debating the University of Oklahoma's interim president David Swank about just how far a university will go before cracking down on its coach and football program. Swank had been the dean of the Oklahoma law school, and he was not, he claimed, a candidate to be the full-time president of the university. Therefore, it seemed to me, he should have felt no need to mince his words about controlling his renegade football club, one that in less than two months had had members arrested for shooting, alleged gang rape, and the sale of cocaine to an undercover FBI agent.

Swank stated, however, that everything was pretty much under control at Bud Wilkinson Hall, that the crimes were "isolated incidents," that head coach Barry Switzer was not going to be fired, but that if there were any more transgressions by anyone on his team or staff, Switzer might get the heave-ho. One month before the crimes the Sooners were placed on three years' probation by the NCAA for "major violations," which included offering cash and cars to recruits and giving airline tickets to players. The NCAA Committee on Infractions stated that for "at least several years, the university has failed to exercise appropriate institutional control" over the football program. One more violation in the next five years and the program would get the NCAA "death penalty," a complete shutdown of the football program for an indefinite amount of time, the same punishment received by Southern Methodist, the only team ever to go to the NCAA gallows. But Swank thought things were on the right track at OU.

I said that since it was clear Switzer could withstand almost any ethical turmoil on his team, the only question was, what kind of a won-lost record could he survive?

Moderator Ted Koppel seemed to like that, and he said, "Hold on with the answer, Mr. Swank. Think about that for a moment. We gotta take another quick break . . ."

I figured that while the commercial was running, Swank would come up with a nice, political way of saying that Switzer could lose every game from now till hell froze over as long as he maintained control of his players.

When we came back, Koppel said, "Before the break Rick Telander asked president David Swank of the University of Oklahoma what kind of a record Barry Switzer could bring back and, I guess the thrust of it was, still hold on to his job—was that it, Rick?"

"Yes."

"What do you think, Mr. Swank?"

We waited, Koppel in Washington, D.C., I in Chicago, Swank in Oklahoma City.

"Again," Swank finally said, "I don't see that an excellent athletic program is inconsistent with having a high-quality academic program. I don't know that I can give a won-lost record, but I *can* tell you that we will place emphasis first on academics at the University of Oklahoma . . . We're not going to tolerate people, as you say, being thrown in the slammer. I can't tell you what record should exist."

Koppel looked disgusted.

"You *could* tell me that it doesn't matter to you," he shot back. "That what matters, what is important to you, is what kind of an education those youngsters get, that if [Switzer] comes in with a losing record, but creates good student-athletes, you'll be happy with him. You could say that."

Swank had a weak smile. "Well, again, I want a top-quality athletic program . . ."

And then it was over.

As I watched the show later on my VCR at home, I was struck by a few things. First, I look like a humorless dolt on TV. But beyond that, I had to marvel at Swank's refusal to say he'd accept a losing record. I figured Oklahoma fans wouldn't be thrilled by a lousy record; after all, they'd almost ridden Switzer out of town when his teams went 7-4-1, 8-4, and 8-4 from 1981 to 1983. But the college president? It was plain that he was afraid that if he publicly lowered the expectations placed on Sooner football teams, the board of regents would string him up like a bad coyote.

I also wondered why Swank was making such a big deal about academics in this matter. Classwork didn't seem to have much to do with anything here. We were talking about jail terms, not midterms. That is not to imply that education isn't an important part of going to college, only that it didn't apply in this situation. Indeed, the year before Switzer had bragged to me about how many Oklahoma football players were getting their degrees and making the dean's list and how all-American tight end Keith Jackson had graduated in less than four years. Jackson, of course, later admitted to taking improper gifts and money from alumni while at OU, but justified it by saying, "Football is a business and that includes college football. When you shut down Oklahoma, you're hurting the business all around the nation." Jackson and I used to have some nice chats—he plays the cello and we'd talk about how badly his fingers could get crunched up before it would affect his playing—and he clearly was a funny guy who had a pretty good notion about the nature of college football. In truth, Oklahoma football players have more mandatory tutoring sessions, study halls, and paid graduate assistants to walk them to class (the g.a.'s lead the players to the buildings and, according to Switzer, "eyeball" them into the classrooms) than any group of college students should have. In our story in *Sports Illustrated* concerning the Sooners' troubles, Bob Sullivan and I had written that it was "no longer clear whether the athletes are pampered royalty or well-attended prisoners who must perform for their keepers."

No, all the business about education was just a red herring thrown out by Swank to draw attention away from the real problem—the hypocrisy of the big-time game. Oklahoma's concern wasn't that the players had done wrong, but that they had raised a ruckus off the field, they had dared to make noise when they weren't supposed to. This thing wasn't about reform, it was about embarrassment. It only underscored the coach's need to bring in great athletes regardless of their character or readiness for college, keep them calm for a few years, win with them, and thus keep his job.

Coaches are forced to give lip service to the shrine of education because they operate out of educational facilities. But their concern is fraudulent. I remember so well one of the assistant coaches at Northwestern who told our star linebacker, "Anybody can be a nuclear physicist, all you have to do is read them books, but it takes a man to play football." They don't need well-rounded, erudite student-athletes who can converse on any subject; they need players who can knock your hat off. They need winners. It is not in their best interests for their players to go to class or even read the papers, except as needed to keep them eligible, and they know this. Thus, regardless of what they may say, they are suspicious of any player who gets too involved in studies, particularly those in the liberal arts or nonlinear types of study. A kid who is hitting the books too hard won't be hitting as hard on the field. I can state from personal experience that the thunderclap revelations and mental proddings received in college classes are not conducive to the backpedal or the recognition of pro-set formations. The more I progressed in my abstract thinking process, the more difficult it sometimes became to shed those thoughts once practice began. I remember well standing and waiting for my unit to be called for half-line passing drills, drifting a million miles away pondering the role of alienation in modern literature. I also remember one of my teammates acting oddly morose for a week or so; only later after we had a couple of beers did I find it was because he had felt compelled to take on the persona of Dr. Bernard Rieux from Camus's *The Stranger,* which he was studying at the time.

Getting an education isn't an important part of a football player's training, particularly if that player has the tools to play in the NFL. Temple's Paul Palmer avoided class whenever possible, but he still finished second in the 1986 Heisman Trophy voting and was taken in the first round by the Kansas City Chiefs. Likewise, running back Brent Fullwood of Auburn went to class about as often as a pet gerbil and then scored a nine on the Wonderlic Personnel Test, an intelligence test given by the NFL (his score put him twenty-three points under that of the average systems analyst, fourteen points under the average meter reader, eleven under the average football player, eight under the typical welder, and five under the average custodian), and still he was the first pick of the Green Bay Packers in 1987. Last season Deion Sanders stayed far away from class at Florida State, scored one point below the average janitor on the Wonderlic Test, and then was the fifth player taken in the 1989 draft. (It's interesting to note that under NCAA rules any football player who is declared eligible at the start of a semester remains eligible for the rest of the period, even if he never takes a step into a classroom. Told that Neon Deion hadn't brightened many classrooms during his senior year at FSU, president Bernard Sliger said, "The position I take is that I'll let the athletic director handle the matter . . . just as I would let the dean of any other school handle similar situations." That made Florida State athletic director C. W. "Hootie" Ingram the dean of—what? The School of Football?)

Other 1989 high first-round picks who didn't set the world of academia on fire include Michigan State offensive tackle Tony Mandarich (fifteen on the Wonderlic), Heisman winner Barry Sanders (sixteen), and Nebraska linebacker Broderick Thomas (ten). Coaches who urge their players to study hard have to know that their words are undermined by the reality of what players see around them. It's nice that they sometimes try to keep alive the fiction that college football had something to do with college, but their recruitment of these obviously academically borderline players (to be charitable) reveals their true views. Indeed, coaches have to say and do so many things they don't believe that it's a wonder they aren't all babbling schizophrenics.

Charley Pell, who was fired four years ago as the University of Florida coach in the wake of an NCAA investigation, said last fall that he had a secret agreement with school president Marshall Criser to accept blame for all the NCAA charges, including things he didn't even know about, to lessen turmoil at the school. But just when you start to feel sorry for these fall guys, you hear about an Earle Bruce. Bruce, who was coldly let go by Ohio State after the 1987 season, eliciting great sympathy from sports journalists, walked out on Northern Iowa in 1988 with three years left on a four-year contract to skip to Colorado State. You investigate and you find the little man pulled the same stunt on the University of Tampa a decade ago.

Add to the roster of these men of integrity the name of Hayden Fry of Iowa, who said last season that he is a fervid opponent of the proposal from some coaches to add a twelfth regular-season game to the schedule. "I'm not in favor of a twelfth game when it sounds like we're just playing for the almighty dollar," he said. One had to wonder if that meant Fry would return all the money Iowa received for playing twelfth games against Hawaii in 1984 and 1988 and against Tennessee in the 1987 Kickoff Classic. Or we can look to the University of Colorado, where at least two dozen players have been arrested in the last three years for crimes ranging from trespassing and assault to burglary and serial rape, and head coach Bill McCartney went on TV last winter to vigorously defend the quality of his program. "Three conditions were attached to my hiring seven years ago," he said with a straight face. "They were, one, not breaking any NCAA rules; two, graduating football players; and three, making the program competitive. Our program has lived up to these requirements." And he is absolutely right. He is just lucky that crime doesn't break any

NCAA rules or he wouldn't have enough players to hold a scrimmage.

And to top things off, we have Louisiana State head coach Mike Archer, whose fullback, Victor Jones, was arrested by state police for driving 123 miles an hour. Archer didn't discipline Jones, pointing out that there is no team rule against speeding. "He told me he was trying to get some bad gas out of his tank," said the good coach. "I believe him."

Have we gone clear through the looking glass and into the land of jabberwocky? Are coaches just grotesque cartoon figures sent on stage to make us laugh with cynical derision? People say, hey, Rick, why don't you kick back and enjoy the show, stop all the complaining. I've tried, believe me, but it doesn't work. There is some real mischief being done in the realm of college football, a lot of it by coaches, and it can't be ignored. If I learned anything at all from playing the game, it is that once you enter the arena, you ought to give 100 percent. Which I intend to do, because, trusting I'm in the arena.

The head coaches are the ones who set the tone for any program, but the assistants, the position coaches, are the ones who can really mess with your head. They are the ones who grade your films, who sit through meetings with you, who know your every quirk, who whisper into your earhole while the head coach is high above in his tower or roving in a golf cart.

Last fall I wrote an article for *Sports Illustrated* about Tommy Chaikin, a former star nosetackle at South Carolina who nearly lost his mind and his life to anabolic steroid abuse. Tommy got big and strong and mean from taking the drugs—he grew from 220 to 270 pounds, increased his bench press to 500 pounds, and sometimes had visions of tearing people's limbs off—but he also became physically and mentally ill. One day in the fall of 1987, the heart palpitations, anxiety attacks, paranoia, and depression became too much for him and he locked himself in his dorm room and placed a cocked and loaded .357 magnum under his chin. He was saved by his father, and after time spent in the psych ward at a Maryland hospital and then resting at home, he got his degree from South Carolina in the spring of 1988. He's okay now, though he's still not 100 percent.

As we sat working on the story, I was shocked by the physical horrors Tommy related. But the worst abuse was the way his position coach, defensive-line coach Jim Washburn, who had tacitly approved of Tommy's steroid use, continued to play with Tommy's mind, to work on his insecurities, even when Tommy was clearly deranged. By the end Tommy had reached the point where he was having anxiety attacks that were so severe he could not move, that made him feel so unbearably out of control that he thought constantly of committing suicide to end the pain. He could not distinguish colors any longer, but saw the whole world in faded, terrifying blurs of light and shadow. Against East Carolina in his third year at South Carolina he had an angina attack, a pre–heart attack condition marked by chest pains, numbness in the arms and chills. Paramedics cut off his jersey and took him in an ambulance to the hospital where a doctor told him his blood pressure readings were off the charts. It was clear that Chaikin was beset with severe emotional and physical problems, and yet linebacker coach Washburn continued to goad him to get Chaikin to play even harder. "He would start others to get me riled up," says Chaikin. "He would scream at me if I made a mistake and tell me I was no good. He would say strange things like, 'Ever think of just ripping someone's head off?' He was hung up on being macho."

I asked Tommy if he didn't hate Washburn for what he had done to him, and he said no. He shrugged. Washburn was a coach, what do you expect?

When I was done writing the rough draft of the story, I traveled to Columbia, South Carolina, to check facts with the Gamecock coaching staff and certain players, to give them their chance to deny or augment Tommy's tale. I went into Joe Morrison's icily air-conditioned office, where the head coach sat motionless, chain-smoking. I asked him questions about Tommy, whom he hardly seemed to remember. He seemed to have remembered very little about anything. He was aloof, distracted, emotionless, bored. Tommy had told me Morrison had had open heart surgery a couple years before and that a doctor had said that if Morrison didn't quit smoking and start taking care of himself, he'd be dead in a year or two. Three months after our meeting, Morrison was dead of a heart attack, at age fifty-one.

I went in to see Washburn, a large man in his thirties with bright red hair and pale-blue eyes, and I knew as I looked at him that he knew that his life would never be the same.

I asked him if he'd encouraged any of his players to take steroids.

''My position as a coach is the same as it's always been,'' he said. ''I'm opposed to them.''

I asked him if he knew Tommy Chaikin was on steroids.

''I didn't know anything for sure, but I suspected him.''

Then I asked him if he remembered holding Tommy's hand before a game to help Tommy fight the pain as the team doctor injected the player's big-toe joint with Xylocaine. Washburn said he didn't. I asked him if he had used steroids during his own playing career.

''I'm not going to get into my past,'' he said. Then he leaned forward and pointed to a photo on his desk of two young kids.

''Besides these children right here, the players I coach are the most important people to me,'' he said with passion. ''I really care.''

We shook hands, and I left to interview other people. A few minutes later Washburn walked into the lounge just off the weight room where I had finished talking with a couple of players.

''You know, I've been thinking,'' he said. ''I do remember being in the training room and holding Tommy's hand when they shot his big toe. He was real nervous.'' Washburn looked as though the most important thing in the world for him was to help me nail down facts for my story.

Washburn left South Carolina after the 1988 season and took a job as the defensive-line coach at Purdue. He barely got to work there, though, because in April he resigned after he was indicted on three counts by a South Carolina grand jury; he pled guilty to importing steroids into the state, and charges of dispensing the drugs without prescriptions and conspiring to conduct a program of illegal steroid use by athletes were dropped. I am sorry if Washburn's life has been damaged because of the criminal investigation that began after the Chaikin story appeared in *Sports Illustrated.* I am sorry whenever anybody is hurt; I take no pride in that sort of thing. But I wonder if Washburn realized how close one of those people who is so important to him came to ending up dead on a dormitory floor, partly, I feel, because of the things Washburn did to him.

Last fall I was at UCLA watching quarterback Troy Aikman fire bullets into the fading light of Westwood, standing with Pepper Rodgers, the former UCLA, Kansas, Georgia Tech, and USFL Memphis Showboats head coach. UCLA was practicing for its big game against crosstown rival USC, and head coach Terry Donahue, normally a decent sort, seemed uptight, crabby, stressed-out. Rodgers had hired Donahue years earlier as an assistant at UCLA, and I asked him now why any man would want to be a coach. Why would anybody want to put up with the crap—the media scrutiny, the pressure to win, the long hours, the insecurity, the oppressive knowledge that a group of boys have control of your fate—that coaches put up with?

Rodgers gave me a number of reasons, none of which had enough fiber to stick in my brain.

The next day I ran into Rodgers in the hotel lobby and he stopped me. ''I've been thinking about your question—'Why would anybody be a coach?' '' he said. ''And I can tell you.

Power. That's the reason. There is no other job where you can yell, 'Hit it,' and a hundred men drop to the ground.''

I believe Rodgers—I've seen Walter Camp's words: ''Coaching a football team is the most engrossing thing in the world. It is playing chess with human pawns''—but still I don't believe college coaches understand how much power they truly have, for good and evil, over their players. A football player's sense of achievement, manhood, and self-esteem are so closely bound up in his on-field performance and acceptance by the coach that he will do almost anything to get the coach's approval, including injuring himself or others if the coach so desires.

You almost have to be a college football player to know how strong that need to please the coach is. After a certain point of commitment, quitting is no longer an option for a player, and he gives himself wholly to the game. At that point his coach's disapproval can be like death. If the coach says chop somebody at the knees, the player will do it. If he tells three players to beat on another, even after the player is down, they will do it; Tommy Chaikin did it. If the coach says you are worthless, you believe him. His least suggestions become like commands.

When you are deep in it, football has a momentum that carries you along like a raging river. Tree branches break off in your hands. Life preservers flung from the bank sink before they reach you. Years ago Yale coach T. A. D. Jones told his players, ''Gentlemen, you are about to play football for Yale against Harvard. Never in your lives will you do anything so important.'' Substitute other college names for those two and you have a statement that at some time almost any college player has agreed with.

The ambivalence a former player feels for his coach is rooted in his gradual understanding of the power the coach has over him, even when he is done playing. In my own career the two coaches I liked the most were men who stood out because they were islands of calm amidst the chaos. The first was Tom Peeler, my high school coach during my junior and senior years. He was slow-moving and slow-talking, with a twang that made me think of rocking chairs and whittling. He helped me with basic football skills and somehow made me want to play my best without worrying about failing. He seldom criticized any of our players, though I remember him looking one day at our all-conference guard, who had more determination than agility, and saying after a time, "Son, you're slow as smoke comin' off manure." My lasting image of the coach is of a tall man standing with his arms folded peacefully on his chest, gazing across the field into the central Illinois distance.

The other man was Bob Zeman, my defensive backfield coach during my junior year in college. He had been a tough safety for seven years in the NFL, but he was quiet and almost shy in his approach to coaching. He would clap his hands and nod his head if one of us defensive backs made a nice play, but he said little when we screwed up. Before games he would gather us together and tell us to play our best. Then he would say, "They're going to complete some passes. They always do. Don't worry about it." Just that little statement, that reassurance that life goes on, was enough to free me from fear and let me play.

But the coach I remember most vividly was our linebacker coach in college. He was mean and strange and old-fashioned. He fancied himself an amateur psychologist who could get the most out of a player, or break him trying. He had no jurisdiction over the defensive backs, which made him furious. He'd see us running in circles with our arms out like airplanes, or making duck calls or sticking grass in each other's earholes, and he'd go bananas. "Look at you," he snarled one day at Jack Dustin, the other cornerback. "First you grow long hair, then you grow a dress. You goddamn—*she-boy*."

Each year he'd pick out a couple of his linebackers to humiliate and abuse, as if destroying their pride and self-esteem were his sole purpose as a coach. He would call the unlucky ones communists, saboteurs, charity cases, losers who would never amount to anything in their whole lives. He would call them "prairie shit" and "little sisters of the poor" and challenge them to fight to the death right there on the field. If he sensed the player shrugging off these attacks, he would cannily find a weakness the player could not ignore—his slowness, his lack of size, his social status—and attack that.

One day he stopped punting practice to rail at a player. He was practically foaming at the mouth. "Your mother's a coward, your father's a coward, you're a coward, and you'll always be a coward!" he raged. The player he was attacking already was so lacking in confidence that it seemed that with this tirade he might melt into the ground.

I can forgive the coach, I suppose. I have a harder time forgiving myself. I watched these things happen to my friends. I was a participant. I think about that a lot.

A couple of years ago I went to the University of Michigan in the spring to do some early reporting for the college-preview edition of *SI*. While waiting to see head coach Bo Schembechler, I noticed a familiar form coming down the hallway. Lo and behold, it was Alex Agase. He was working for his old pal Bo as an unpaid assistant for the Wolverines, keeping his hand in the game until heading into the golden years.

We went into his little office and he opened a drawer and pulled out a dog-eared Northwestern game program from 1970. It was open to the page with the players' faces on it. Agase had made little checks next to the players he liked or who were good athletes. My face had a check next to it. He found the pictures of two of our best players, free safety Eric Hutchinson and linebacker John Voorhees, and tapped on them. Hutchinson and Voorhees were brilliant performers, two of the most gifted, instinctive defenders ever to play at Northwestern.

"One thing I still can't figure out," said Agase with a look of befuddlement, "is how two guys who hated the game of football could be so good at it."

He looked at me, and I started to tell him that they didn't hate football. I had roomed with them and I knew. They loved the game. They just hated all the bullshit surrounding it. But I knew he couldn't understand, so I just nodded and let it pass.

Memories ebb and surge.

Every summer my college teammates get together for a two-day party at a resort in Wisconsin. I go along to reminisce and to see the guys, and in certain ways, to come to terms with the past. This last year some of the former players decided we should all get together and pledge $25,000 to fund a football meeting room in the new athletic building being constructed on campus. The room would bear a plaque indicating that we were the donors and dedicating the gift to Alex Agase.

One of the guys asked me if I'd contribute.

I don't know how I feel about a lot of things, and I'm not sure I want Agase to feel like a saint. But after a time, I said I'd do it. What else could I say? The man was my coach.

STRETCHING

There were two football players everybody knew about. They went to different high schools and played different positions, but they both were such dominant players that whenever anyone talked about local ball, they always ended up talking about these two.

Alan went to the high school he'd be going to soon. The school was on the outskirts of town, in what passed for the suburbs. There were cornfields close by and woods beyond that. The school was new and had an indoor swimming pool and acres of grass.

Nick went to the Catholic boys school downtown. It was old and battered and the priests were supposed to be mean. There were no fields at Nick's school and the players had to take a bus to a public park for practice. Nick was a fierce, violent person from a poor family. He'd lost an eye somehow as a boy, and that supposedly was why he was so mean.

Nick lifted weights constantly. He was built like a god. He would walk into the men's room at a dance and tell everybody there not to move until he left. Don't flush, don't shake, don't breathe, he'd say. He'd heard that guys stood frozen at the urinals for a long time after Nick left just to make sure he was gone.

Alan was well built, too. He was a little bit taller than Nick, handsome and an exceptional athlete. His father, however, was rich, and the family lived in one of the town's most elegant homes on a bluff overlooking the river. Alan was an honor-roll student and a first-class citizen. He was president of the student council, man most likely to succeed, and a number of other things like that. His girlfriend was blonde and beautiful, and together they reaped most of the awards the high school had to offer. There was something else he'd heard about Alan. He was nice. Even if you were just a freshman, you supposedly could walk up to him in the hallway and he'd talk to you. In certain ways Alan was Nick's opposite. It seemed odd to him that two people like that could be so good at the same game.

In his dream Alan and Nick met in a park near his house. They each had on their letter jackets and their friends stood in a circle around them. The river flowed silently in the distance. Clouds raced above the trees. Alan and Nick, weaponless except for their bare hands, were going to fight to the death. They revolved and everybody waited. The wind stopped. The clouds disappeared.

And then he would wake up.

Alan and Nick never fought in his dream; they'd always get close, but not close enough. He was sure they never fought in real life, either. And he was glad about that. They were symbols to him, and he wasn't sure symbols should have such clear resolution.

Still, he always wondered who would have won his dream fight. And even more, whom he wanted to win.

CHAPTER 4

A Winning Team Makes a Fortune for Its School

Let's say you're sitting in Memorial Stadium in Lincoln, Nebraska, with 73,649 other people waiting for the University of Nebraska Cornhuskers to barbecue a Big Eight sacrificial lamb. Of course, if there are only 73,650 people in the stands, including yourself, then the stadium is only filled to capacity, which would be a startling event indeed. In 1988, Nebraska averaged 2,692 people over capacity for each of its six home games, which set a new attendance record for the school—by exactly one person per game. (The new ticket manager felt the urge to make his maiden season a memorable one.) But such details are unimportant since Memorial Stadium has been at least sold-out for every game since the Huskers played Missouri on November 3, 1962—a string of 161 straight games that started two years before the Beatles landed in America. And 1989 is already a sellout, and you can bet 1990 will be, too, and 1991 and so on—barring the complete demise of the football program or the perversion of some vital aspect of the Nebraska juggernaut, such as changing the team color from scarlet to blue.

As I sit here in the stadium, all I can see is an undulating sea of red above the turf. Red sport coats, red T-shirts, red dresses, red Stetson hats and ball caps, red windbreakers, red bib overalls, red shoes. There is so much red that my mind loses focus for an instant and I don't know where I am. I could be at the University of Georgia or Ohio State or Alabama or Oklahoma or Arkansas and it would look just like this. Red. This disorientation happens to me more and more at these giant collegiate convocations. It doesn't really matter, in fact, where I am, and I drift with it for a moment. Lincoln, Athens, Columbus, Tuscaloosa, Norman, Fayetteville—the wave of red means a whole lot of green, and beyond the ritual of this gathering and the rising tide of sheer expectation washing over the crowd, it is that cash outlay that strikes me as unique. Why, there must be half a million dollars' worth of scarlet clothes here alone. But it's not so much the clothes that reek of money spent or even the feeling that there are a lot of rich people in the crowd, because there are certainly many poor people, too; it's just this overwhelming sense I get that money is not a big deal to any of these people compared to what it has bought them: bonding, ritual, entertainment, catharsis. The money for tickets, parking, pennants, Herbie Husker hats, $100,000 red land-yachts, whatever, has been spent freely, willingly, joyfully. And the University of Nebraska is the creator of this money splurge. It has produced a football team, as other universities have, that carries so much emotional freight for so many people that it has become an awesome economic force.

It would seem obvious, then, that the universities make lots of money off the presentation of big-time football. In all the wild money-flinging excess there must be buckets of cash that drop right into the coffers of the schools themselves. Certainly this is true. It has to be.

It isn't.

As we have already discussed, the direct cash raised by ticket sales, sky-box rentals, parking passes, and the like bypasses the university and goes to its semiindependent subsidiary, the athletic department. The athletic department then uses that revenue to finance itself, and when possible, to extend its tentacles more securely into the heart of the university by building more structures and increasing its staff and responsibilities so that if there ever should be a downturn in the money generated by the football team (and to a lesser extent, the basketball team, which is the only other revenue-producing sport on campus), the resultant shuttering of gyms or laying off of staff or cutting back on scholarships would seem unfair and socially repugnant and there would be a lot of sympathy for the poor wretches in the athletic department. And sympathy is the next-best thing to cold cash, because sympathy allows athletic departments to concoct more ways to make greenbacks, such as pursuing that twelfth game or getting corporate sponsorship or starting a national tournament. And you'd better believe that athletic directors make wonderful hand-wringers and great impersonators of poor, overburdened administrators just trying to make ends meet.

Texas Christian University athletic director Frank Windegger, who has served on the NCAA Council and is currently on the College Football Association (CFA) Board of Directors and the CFA's Athletic Directors' Committee as well as the National Association of College Directors of Athletics, has already come out proclaiming that big-time football has to add another game to stay solvent. "Sixty-two percent of Division I schools are in deficit budgets," he said last October. "And it's not going to get better on its own. It was a real signal to me when Michigan was two and a half million dollars in the red. You're talking about a team that can put one hundred thousand fans in the stands, and if they can't meet a budget, then what is everyone else supposed to do?"

God, it's so sad, you almost hesitate to ask why Michigan's athletic department can't eke by on its $20-million budget (largest in the land), or why coaches and, golly, athletic directors can't take just one tiny pay cut. But they must have their reasons, and anyway, that's another issue. Let's stick to the university itself here.

The university proper knows better than to ask for any of the football program's money. Reach into that cookie jar and you get your hand hacked off at the wrist. But the school can rightly expect to get some of the trickle-down or overflow or splash-off from the sport, as delirious fans throw their money at the sacred football beast, can't it? Well, no. A great deal of that revenue goes to the surrounding community in the form of restaurant, motel, and souvenir expenditures, which don't benefit the university except as goodwill. Indeed, some college-town businesses would certainly go under if it weren't for the big football weekends on campus. The manager of Beggar's Banquet, a 160-seat restaurant in East Lansing, Michigan, home of Michigan State, told *Air Destinations* magazine recently that MSU's six 1988 football weekends accounted for ten percent of the eatery's total yearly income. "It's an amazing amount when you think about it," the manager said. "We get a lot of return business year after year. One man from Ohio, for example, has had Friday, Saturday, and Sunday reservations for every home game over the last ten years, and usually for ten or twelve people." It has been estimated that if the NCAA death penalty had been inflicted upon the Texas A&M football program last year, the cost to the College Station economy would have been something like $25 million. According to commentary in the *Austin* (Texas) *American-Statesman* in March 1989, the realization of this potential economic disaster "might explain [ex-player] George Smith's mind-boggling confession, stage-managed by the A&M officials who flew him back to College Station on a private jet to save the football team from ruin." Smith, of course, was the former Aggie running back who had first stated that he was given illegal money by coach Jackie Sherrill, then suddenly "confessed" that he had made the whole story up. (The kicker came in April, when Smith told the *Dallas Morning News* that, actually, he had made up *the retraction* in return for promised payment from A&M athletic department officials of "$30,000—in that neighborhood.")

If nothing else, it's easy to see what a tenuous position universities with big-time football programs have put themselves into in relation to their surrounding communities. A protracted losing streak or, God forbid, a shutdown of the program itself could be as unfair to the townsfolk as the laying off of factory workers or the moving of a major plant. Still, what we're trying to nail down here is what's in it for the colleges themselves. Where is *their* cut? After all, if a university is going to profane itself so openly, demonstrate to all that it is nothing but a hypocritical house of platitudes willing to use certain of its young men as unpaid entertainers in a high-stress and dangerous industry while telling them they are nothing but students, it certainly better be getting paid for such embarrassment and degradation. By definition, a whore charges a price; if she didn't, she would no longer be a whore, but a fool.

So—of course!—the money comes in *indirectly* as a result of the football program. That's how it is. It comes seeping in, in the form of grants and endowments and gifts and bequeathals from wealthy alums and fans who have been so smitten with the success or struggles of the football team that they feel compelled to give to the sponsoring institution itself, the university, and not to the athletic department. Not right there on the spot, maybe, but within a reasonable amount of time after the monumental goal-line stand or bowl-game blitz. To the university's general fund. To its math and science and English departments. To its building and housing funds. To its fine-arts center and to the tech lab and the student newspaper and radio and all the other needy aspects of every big school. That's how it happens. Yes? Right?

Wrong.

I hate always to spoil the party, but let's check out the facts, not the perceptions. In the January 13, 1988, *Chronicle of Higher Education,* writer Douglas Lederman states: "Proponents of big-time sports have long held that a visible, successful sports program greatly adds to an institution's financial well-being. They argue that a winning, big-time program attracts students, fosters institutional name recognition, and stimulates state aid and voluntary giving.

"The argument has been repeated with such frequency and certainty that it seems to have become accepted as fact by many.

"But most of the fund-raisers and scholars who have studied the relationship between athletic success and fund-raising are skeptical."

Lederman is nothing if not understated in his appraisal of the athletics–fund-raising connection, though his data shoot large holes in the traditional "facts." Less restrained is Dr. James Frey, our friend from the sociology department at UNLV, who published a study on the matter in the January 1985 edition of *Currents, the Journal of the Council of Advancement and Support of Education*. He states: "The performance of athletic teams, particularly basketball and football, is purported to stimulate financial donations to general university development efforts, especially from alumni. Athletic programs are also viewed as a vehicle to attract nonalumni and otherwise disinterested constituencies to the campus in order to create a sense of attachment that can be 'converted' to a financial contribution to the institution's academic fund. . . .

"While we want to believe that the above is an accurate assessment, it has to be concluded that the common beliefs about the relation of athletic success and voluntary contribution are based on casual observation rather than systematic analysis. When subjected to closer scrutiny, much of what we believe to be true about this relationship is, in fact, false. . . . Within the last decade there have been a number of empirical examinations of the relation of athletic success to fund-raising outcomes. The basis conclusion . . . is that there is no relation between athletic success and any measure of voluntary financial contributions. In fact, it is pointed out that athletic success often has the opposite effect—it depresses contributions."

Frey then shows a chart summarizing the studies done by researchers on the relation between athletic success and university fund-raising results. The first study, from 1934, sampled sixteen football schools and sixteen nonfootball schools and showed that endowments were actually higher for the schools that did not emphasize athletics. The rest of the studies, a dozen all told, covering hundreds of institutions over a fifty-year period and reported by different researchers, mostly told variations on the same theme. "Dropping football did not have negative impact on alumni donation." "Athletic performance is not a motivator of alumni giving." "No positive impact of athletic success on any measure. Also, no effect on enrollment." "Some evidence that [athletic] success depresses giving." "General body of alumni rated athletics ninth on funding priority scale. . . . Both the general body and leaders rated athletic events low on 'most-remembered experience.' " "No evidence to support relationship between athletic performance and any measure of giving. Some indication of negative effect." "Strong relation between football success and donation to athletic programs. No relation between athletic success and alumni donation to annual fund."

Frey then makes a rather obvious observation: "If athletic programs are having difficulty raising their own monies, it seems incredulous to expect these same activities to produce funds for the institution." But then one always hears the argument that football fans will become donors to the academic side of the school once they take that autumn walk across campus and see the library and classrooms and statues of scholars. On this matter, Frey quotes development director Richard Conklin of Notre Dame, who says, "We at Notre Dame have had extensive experience trying to turn athletic interests of 'subway alumni' to development purposes—and we have had no success." Conklin adds, "There is no evidence that the typical, nonalumnus athletic fan of Notre Dame has much interest in its educational mission."

In his article in *The Chronicle of Higher Education,* Lederman quotes P. Warren Heemann, the vice president for development at Georgia Tech, as saying, "So much of the big money for colleges and universities comes from bequests and other large gifts. The vagaries of the football team, its ups and downs, will not affect those big gifts. People who make big gifts do so in support of the academic, instructional program, not a sports team." Roger Olson, vice president for development at Southern Cal, agrees, saying, "The bulk of our fund-raising would be intact with or without athletics."

Lederman quotes Notre Dame's Conklin one more time. "There isn't any correlation between giving at Notre Dame and athletic success," he says, pointing to the recent, unsuccessful five-year tenure of overmatched football coach Gerry Faust. "We raised more money during the Gerry Faust era than during any other period in the university's history. What does that tell you?"

What it tells us all is that if a philanthropist is going to give to the library, it is because he loves books, not buttonhooks—even at the Golden Dome, where one would suspect that football means more to college supporters than at any other university in the land. But the point has been demonstrated again and again and is now almost beyond dispute: *Big-time sport and support for learning have nothing to do with one another.* At Tulane, for instance, donations rose by $5 million a year after the university dropped its big-time basketball program in 1985. At Wichita State, which dropped its football program in 1986, enrollment climbed by 200 in 1987 and university giving nearly doubled, jumping from just under $13.5 million to almost $26 million in that year.

And the final irony here is that, though a good sports reputation doesn't help a university, a bad one can certainly cause it one very big headache. I have often wondered what good winning a slew of football games did for SMU. A few loudmouthed Texas braggarts got to whoop and holler about how their boys could whip up on those Aggies and Owls and Horned Frogs in the Southwest Conference, but the football program got the death penalty and the school's rich kids got to wear black-humor T-shirts that read, "SMU—Ponies, Porsches, Probation." Beyond that? A lot of embarrassment for the faculty, the serious students, the alumni, the governor of Texas, and the entire state.

I talked to Professor Frey about all of this. I knew what he had written in various journals, but I wondered what his own nonacademic feelings were, since he himself works out of a school that, as far as anyone in America can tell, consists of a few buildings across from Circus Circus, a couple of blackjack tables, and a basketball team. What is it like, I wanted to know, to teach at a place that seemed to exist only as a front for Jerry Tarkanian and the Runnin' Rebels?

Frey laughed. "It's the same as it is at many other places," he said. "When you're a relatively new institution—we're only about thirty years old here—or you're relatively obscure, like, say, the University of Arkansas at Little Rock, then sometimes you decide that the way to get recognition and financial attention is to push your sports program. When a school is on the make like that, sometimes you can produce a good image-return—temporarily. But what happens, if your sports team is successful—and I've warned schools about this—is that you draw the attention of the NCAA and you get scrutinized and then you get into trouble. Then you've got a negative image. And we're not even talking about money, because we know that relationship to sports success. But now you have a sports reputation that you have to *live down*. We're sick of it here. And you know what—they're sick of it at a lot of schools with big sports programs. And what's unfair here at UNLV is that the academics have really blossomed, but nobody knows that."

Frey went on to explain that Tarkanian's recruiting of troubled New York basketball phenom Lloyd Daniels, a young man with a drug problem whom Frey believed to be functionally illiterate, only reinforced the public's image of UNLV as an outlaw school. As we spoke, Daniels, who had been made the legal ward of UNLV assistant basketball coach Mark Warkentien, was lying in a Mary Immaculate Hospital bed in Jamaica, Queens, in critical condition with three bullet wounds suffered in a drug-related incident.

"The presidents have never really understood the athletic department," Frey continued. "The coaches have no connection with the university. And the presidents are not willing to act against this elite financial and booster coalition because it might compromise their own political support. The cult of the celebrity coach is a real problem. You can't challenge certain scams because the personal interests of the coach override organizational concerns. The coaches are leading community figures—Switzer, Paterno, previously men like John Wooden and Bear Bryant—they're better known than anybody. We have one here. Tarkanian has his own fan club, a gift shop at the airport, a place called Tarkanian's Sports Club, the gym is called The Shark Tank.

"The faculty isn't equipped to deal with things like this, either. They express consternation, but they don't take action. Coaches are beyond them. I remember one time the football coach came in to talk to the faculty, and I thought one professor was going to pee in his pants. He thought you didn't talk to coaches. So what the faculty does, because it is somewhat baffled and feels powerless, is just say that big-time sport is not a part of university life—I'll ignore it, it's not legitimate, I'll give it no quarter; I'll just treat it as a crass entertainment vehicle, but it won't affect my personal life or my research here.

"I like sports and I go to the games, but I'm thinking about turning in my season tickets for next year. It's hard to fathom. It's so complex, so convoluted, that it's hard to figure what to do. But things are getting worse."

Think about what the pursuit of football victories has done for the University of Oklahoma. On a national level, it has made the school a laughingstock, a caricature of a greedy, low-minded hick institution that can find satisfaction only in beating somebody at a violent game, sort of like a hillbilly who just loves wrasslin' fellers till they cry, "Uncle!" Remember the famous and oft-repeated quote from Dr. George L. Cross, the Oklahoma president in the fifties who said, "We want to build a university our football team can be proud of"? Dr. Cross now regrets that comment, says, in fact, that it was stated sarcastically to shake some lazy senators out of their torpor and get them to appropriate some money to the school's general fund so that the educational process at OU could rival the gridiron steamroller. "It all makes me sick," Dr. Cross told Ira Berkow of the *New York Times* this winter as he considered the mess the football program and school now found itself in. "But it's not just Oklahoma's problems. What's happening here at the moment symbolizes with specifics what's wrong with big-time college athletics, particularly football." The eighty-four-year-old Cross, retired since 1968, then reflected on the past. "I remember how all of it started here. It was 1945 and the war had ended, and here in Oklahoma we were still feeling very depressed from those tough days that Steinbeck wrote about in *The Grapes of Wrath.* At a board of regents meeting, it was suggested to me that I try to get a good football team. It would give Oklahomans a reason to have pride in the state. And it did, but I don't think it was very good for the university."

So how did this incorrect notion about athletics and fund-raising get started in the first place? Why do college people still push for athletic success as if it had some sort of pot-of-gold payoff to the university? I marveled when I saw recently that the University of South Alabama placed an ad in the *NCAA News* offering a reward of $5,000 for anyone who could come up with information that could help the school keep forward Gabe Estaba eligible for another year of varsity basketball, even though Estaba had apparently used up his four years of allotted playing time. The pure mercenary aspect of such an offer floored me.

Did the school think that the five grand was an investment it would recoup if Estaba played one more year? Or was there someone in the school's administration who figured it was good publicity and would draw some gift money to the school itself? And then I saw that Senator J. Bennett Johnston of Louisiana said that he would introduce legislation to prevent college athletes from signing pro football or basketball contracts before their classes graduate. In other words, he would make athletes indentured servants to their universities. His proposition is so unethical and, it seems to me, so patently illegal that it's hard to figure a justification for even proposing such a bill. Then it appears: The senator says that his bill was inspired by speculation that Louisiana State basketball star guard Chris Jackson, a freshman all-American, might quit school to turn pro. The humble senator merely wanted his trained dog to keep performing for him and continue bringing in all that alleged revenue to the coffers of the state institute of higher learning.

Oh, my, the deeper we go the darker it gets. In truth, the purported money-making aspect of athletics goes back to earlier days when boosters—businessmen who "boosted" various college programs with funding—decided that one way to promote their communities as optimistic, growth-oriented places worthy of political and capital investment was to boost the athletic programs of the colleges in their area. Boosters very quickly gained basic (if somewhat hidden) control of athletic departments simply because of the money that they could supply to, or withhold from, the programs. Many boosters, in fact, have traditionally been members of the board of regents of the schools they support or members of other powerful policy-making groups in the community. And since these men were mostly successful businessmen used to winning, dominating, and getting what they wanted, they pushed hard for the teams to be the best they could be without much regard to the academic aspects of the universities. Because these men controlled so much money themselves, they were able to convince the universities that what they did for the athletic departments was also in the best interest of the schools. When it became obvious that this was no longer the case, if it ever had been, the administrators of the schools felt they didn't have enough power to make any changes in the existing athletic structure. Either that or they liked things the way they were, despite the fraudulent nature of the relationship.

Mostly, though, they were, and are, afraid. Jan Kemp, the coordinator of developmental studies English at the University of Georgia and a woman who has seen the corruption of that school's football program from close range, recently wrote, "Education harbors too many scared people. By example, our schools teach fear and love of money, the primary fear being the loss of money." And that is true. But again, the amazing thing here is that these money-worshiping college presidents won't even attack their football programs with the ammunition that's already in the barrels of their guns: FOOTBALL TEAMS DON'T MAKE MONEY FOR THE SCHOOL. They have to know this. The reports I have cited should be no secret to college administrators. I mean, who reads *The Chronicle of Higher Education* if not higher educators?

But as Frey writes, "Old myths die hard. We want to believe athletics produce revenue. If they do not, what then remains for the justification of athletic programs on a campus? If we assert that athletics no longer fulfill an educational role, if the personality development of the participants is irrelevant, if athletic notoriety is adverse to academic interests, and if athletics can't produce revenue, what good is an athletic program?"

Even as I was pondering the answer to that question I read in the paper something that seemed to undermine the entire well-documented premise that sports does not bring money to a school. In early May, millionaire entrepreneuers and Notre Dame graduates Edward J. DeBartolo and Edward J. DeBartolo, Jr., (the owners of the Pittsburgh Penguins and the San Francisco 49ers, respectively) donated $33 million to Notre Dame. The bequest, the eighteenth-largest ever to a university and the largest in history to Notre Dame or any Catholic university, looked to be a direct result of the elation men like the DeBartolos must have felt over the undefeated 1989 national champion Irish football team. Surely, two men whose lives revolve around sports felt the urge to give after getting their adrenaline cranked up by Lou Holtz's boys. That being the case, it could be argued that the Notre Dame football team has become one of the premier university fund-raisers of all time.

I called Notre Dame to see if my analysis was correct, to see if all the research I had done had been undone by a single act of largesse. Sports information director John Heisler picked up the phone, and moments later associate athletic director Roger Valdiserri got on the same line. Both of them are old friends of mine, and I asked them rather casually if, perhaps, the DeBartolos' gift had risen like an angel from the glorious clouds of the national title.

"Nope," said Heisler. "This has been in the making for at least eight years. With a gift this large, working out the details takes a lot of time." I thought back. That meant the germ of the gift was planted in the gloomy soil of the Faust years. What a catalyst that man was!

But all the money was going to support athletics, wasn't it?

"None of it," said Heisler. "Sixteen million is for classrooms. Fourteen million for the performing arts building. And three million for a men's quadrangle."

"It has nothing at all to do with football," chimed in Valdiserri. "If anything, it's creating a dilemma for the football program. The construction will take away two huge parking areas for football games."

He added that the DeBartolos' contribution was just part of a three-year capital fund drive called A Strategic Moment, which also had nothing to do with promoting or giving to the football program, but which now had a nice little kitty of $417 million attached to it. Happy times in South Bend. The men fairly cackled with fund-raisers' glee.

So once again, the premise held. And I thought again of the professor's question: If, on top of everything else bad that big-time sport does to a university, it can't produce revenue, ''what good is an athletic program?''

There aren't a whole lot of answers to that question. In fact, there's only one. Want to sit back and let the college presidents wrestle with it for a while?

STRETCHING

It was homecoming and he was running around left end. The pitch man was open out on the wing, but one of his options was to keep the ball himself, and he had. One tackler missed him.

He didn't have the greatest arm and his hand fakes weren't all that nifty, but he was a good athlete and a decent runner. He had been made the quarterback because of that and because the coach felt he was a leader. The all-state quarterback had graduated last spring, leaving this vacancy. The coach had put him here and told him to run the show. He loved running the show. As he stood behind center, he liked the fact that all the players, all the people in the stadium, were waiting for him to do something. He thought how nice it would be to draw that out forever.

He spun and then somebody hit him. The tackler's helmet rose up under his chin, and he saw stars briefly. At the end of the quarter he came to the bench and took off his helmet. His chinguard was soaked with blood.

His team won the game by three touchdowns, mostly because the other team had a poor offense and a badly-confused defense.

He got dressed and his father drove him to the emergency room where he got eight stitches in his chin. The only time it hurt much was when the idiot doctor decided to scrub out the cut with a toothbrush. He'd spent a lot of time waiting, so when he finally got out of the hospital, it was too late to see his buddies, and he had to go home to bed.

The next night was the homecoming dance. He picked up his date in his dad's car. He had on a sport coat and a carnation and, of course, a bandage on his chin. His date wore a dress that made her look like a woman. In the backseat were his buddy, the tight end, and his buddy's date. She was nice looking, but his own date was the prettiest girl in school. She wasn't the homecoming queen, but she should have been. She'd be the prom queen in May.

They got to the dance and walked in. There were huge fish on the walls of the gym. There was an underwater theme to the dance, which, because they were in the middle of the corn belt, seemed particularly exotic to them. They walked around and looked at the decorations. The score of the game was posted on one wall in huge green numerals, and there were several banners praising the football team or describing the beating it had given its opponent. A drawing of him throwing the ball was featured on one poster.

He noticed girls looking at his date as they walked out onto the basketball court to dance. Boys looked at her, too, and then they looked at him. What he saw in their eyes was that they wanted to be him.

He was the quarterback, the victorious, gracious, injured quarterback at the homecoming dance with the prettiest girl in school. He tried with all his might to appreciate that.

CHAPTER 5

Football Is Play

All through the course of the cataclysmic 1988 college football season, Steve Robinson and I kept talking, trying to come up with stories for the magazine.

Of course, we'd get to Barry Sanders, if he kept running up his totals the way he was. And somebody would do Troy Aikman, and probably Rodney Peete and maybe Tony Rice. I suggested all-American wide receiver Hart Lee Dykes, just because he'd been able to put four schools on probation, and I guess because I like his name. I'm into athletes' names, and I've told Steve that. I keep lists of good ones. I just rip them out of papers or programs or whatever they might be in, throw them into my briefcase, then paste them onto my master list when I get home. Tyrone Shoulders, Furmia Nealy, Erskine Sankey, Oudious Lee. I read them to myself the way little boys read their baseball cards. Admiral Dewey Larry, a cornerback from UNLV. I. M. Hipp, Jarvis Redwine, Wonderful Monds, Jr.—all running backs from Nebraska. Redonia Duck, out of Fairleigh-Dickinson, a basketball player. Flenoil Crook from New Mexico. Cestrakiah Lewis from Lamar Tech. Levertus Larry, Algee Lovelace, Loranzo Square, Lorenzo Distant, Goliath Yeggins—from all over the place. Notre Dame's D'Juan Francisco and his brother, Hiawatha. Also Raghib and Qadry Ismail, Notre Dame and Syracuse, respectively. And that great old NFL wide receiver duo—Jubilee Dunbar and Fair Hooker, traded one for the other, straight up, name for name. Later I would think about Roosevelt Snipes, the former Florida State star running back, but that was when I was down in Sarasota in April and I read in the local paper that Snipes was being held in the Sarasota County jail on charges of robbery and resisting arrest, with bond set at $25,769. He had been out of jail on bond for other unrelated charges including robbery, criminal mischief, and resisting arrest, and well, that was one great name that had come to a sorry state.

I suggested doing something on this kid I had heard about, Walter Herring, a defensive back at Southeast Missouri. He was the youngest child in a family of twenty-nine. Steve thought that was amusing—we discussed the line of questioning I should take regarding hand-me-downs, food, living-room wrestling matches, and bathroom privileges at the Herring homestead. But what we had to cover, obviously, were the best players first, then the interesting ones.

Tony Mandarich's name came up, the giant offensive tackle from Michigan State. I had just finished working on the piece with South Carolina's Tommy Chaikin about his descent into the maelstrom of steroid abuse, and I told Steve that as far as I could tell, Mandarich was a walking steroid container and I didn't see how, in all good conscience, I could write about the guy after having taken a rock-solid stance against the drugs. Steve agreed. We didn't know if Mandarich had ever so much as sniffed a steroid, but you have to draw the line somewhere. At 6′6″ and a tapered 320 pounds, Mandarich *looked* like he used steroids. It's a pitiful comment on the business to judge people that way, but what is a writer supposed to do?

I think back on the times I've been burned. I remember writing a feature on Memphis State basketball player Keith Lee and asking him if he was bought off to go to Memphis State, and how he said, no, he got no money, wasn't offered anything, blah, blah, blah, and how I took his word for it and wrote an upbeat piece. Then it came out not long after that, yep, he was given cash to go there. Then I wrote about running backs Pete Johnson and Chuck Muncie of the San Diego Chargers, the "Baby Elephant Backfield," and those two heavyweights assured me that they were off pot and coke and fully dedicated to the game. And I believed them, even though Muncie was sitting on a bench at training camp in La Jolla in his practice uniform, twitching and smoking cigarettes like a fiend, and Johnson weighed 285 pounds and looked to me like a guy who just stumbled out of a saloon; and not too long after that Johnson got busted in a drug deal and Muncie got nailed in a separate deal; Pete was acquitted of all charges, but as I write this, Chuck is five months into a two-and-a-half-year sentence at the Metropolitan Corrections Center in San Diego. Then before the 1987 Orange Bowl I wrote a piece on University of Miami middle linebacker George Mira, Jr. He is the son of former Miami all-American quarterback George Mira, Sr., a nice study in the father-son genetic chain, I figured, a normal kind of kid who grew up just down the street from my house in Key West. Georgie had gotten into some trouble with the Miami cops earlier in the year, and they had found a vial of steroids in his truck. I asked him about the steroids and he swore they belonged to a sick non-football-playing friend of his, that he never took steroids. His father backed him up. So I believed them and wrote a nice profile, and then a year later, before the 1988 Orange Bowl, Georgie flunked the pregame drug urinalysis, testing positive for a diuretic commonly used by steroid takers to mask the presence of the steroids. Mira told me he took the diuretic because he had eaten a lot of salty food recently and felt bloated and didn't know the type of diuretic he took was a banned drug, anyway. And I believed him again.

Well, maybe I didn't believe him. But I wanted to. I did
want to think that he was lying. I still don't. Most people think
sportswriters get their kicks from exposing the failings of would-be heroes. We don't. We want heroes, too. Oh, dear, do we want them. But we want the truth more than that, and when the truth is bad too many times we turn cynical, in defense.

So I didn't write about Mandarich for the entire year. He had a stupendous 1988 season, devastating opposing defenses the way no offensive lineman ever has. I watched the highlights of the Michigan State–Iowa game on ESPN and saw him block linebacker Jim Reilly five yards off the line, stick his hand under Reilly's face mask, drive the poor man's head backward, and plant him into the turf like a dog burying a bone. But I was already starting to lose it big time, and I told Steve there was no way I could write about this guy. I just couldn't. My ethical compass was spinning wildly. Steve understood.

Then the season was over and the NFL draft was coming. Mandarich passed his drug tests at the Gator Bowl and at the scouting combine in Indianapolis. At the private workout he held for scouts at Michigan State, he blew the strength, speed, and agility tests off the charts. He ran the forty in 4.65, broad-jumped an astounding 10′3″, benched 225 pounds thirty-nine times, and leaped vertically 30 inches. It was the highest-rated workout of any pro prospect on earth in 1989. I called Michigan State coach George Perles just to check the numbers and get a feel for the beast. "It was something to see," said Perles. "Goddamn, we got the whole thing on tape." The coach guaranteed Mandarich didn't use steroids, either. "This is a different player," he said. "We'll never see another."

Mandarich was going to go no lower than the second player in the draft, behind Aikman. That was certain. He might even go first, in front of everybody—quarterbacks, Heisman winners, you name it. Either way, he would be one of the highest-drafted offensive lineman ever, the highest-drafted Canadian citizen ever (he's from Ontario), and certainly one of the most ever drafted at any position. He was sports of my failing will, we had to do him. *Sports* ...ed that to its readers. I told Steve that, well, all ...what the hell, I'll do the guy, do him with vigor and an open mind. I might as well take the bull by the horns and hang on for one last ride.

So there I sit in March at the juice bar at the Powerhouse Gym in East Lansing when Mandarich walks in and says he is ready to hoist some iron. He has already dropped out of school, and despite four and a half years of study he is still seventeen credits short of a degree. But book-learning has about as much to do with his future as piano-tuning does. He takes off his "All-Madden Team" sweatshirt (he is the only player ever to make John Madden's all-pro team while still in college) to reveal a ripped T-shirt that reads, "Fuck the NCAA." He'd been suspended for three games by the NCAA for simply writing to the NFL during the summer and inquiring about its supplemental draft, so I understand his sentiment, more or less. A gold crucifix hangs down between the pectorals of his 60-inch (expanded) chest like a gilded paper clip between two pigs. I have seen larger and heavier and taller human beings, but something about Mandarich just seems overwhelmingly . . . *massive*. I can't take my eyes off him. Arms like stovepipes, a little boy's face, thinning hair, a tattoo of a dagger and a rose bleeding green Spartan blood down his ankle above the words "Never Surrender," knee wraps that read "Die Bitch," a baseball cap perched backward on his head, a courteous, reserved, yet somehow terrifying demeanor —it is hard to tell who or what this guy is. Part of the intrigue is that there is no way to tell how much of his musculature is real, weight-trained, or chemically induced. There is no way to tell how much of *him* is real, either.

He walks behind the bar and cranks up the throttle on the Guns n' Roses tape in the sound system. He informs me, yelling, that the Powerhouse used to be a disco called The Outer

Limits, and I trust him. Large speakers ring the ceiling of the gym like bazookas in a gun nest, aimed at our heads.

As W. Axl Rose screeches, "I used to love her/But I had to kill her," Mandarich starts his prelifting ritual. He rubs Icy Hot liniment on his shoulders, wraps supports around his wrists, and starts to jack himself up with caffeine. He drinks a 16-ounce bottle of Super Tea, a potion that, according to its label, contains 340 calories and "maximum caffeine." Then he downs 32 ounces of coffee. He has already taken a Vivarin tablet—200 milligrams of caffeine—and in no time he is bouncing his knees, drumming his fingers on his thighs, grinding his teeth. He lifts weights twice a day, every day except one in an eight-day cycle, so the ritual is nothing new for him. For me it's kind of intense. He bought me a bottle of Super Tea, I drank it, and now I'm halfway wired myself.

"If you're not going to be intense," Mandarich says with a grin as he rises to punish some heavy metal, "why come in?"

His lifting partner is a tiny thing named Rob "Buck" Smith. Actually, Smith is just short, 5′ 4″, not tiny. He weighs 185 pounds, and he's shaved and tanned and bulging with muscles like the competitive body-building freak he is. Still, next to Mandarich, who only has shaved arms and lightly stubbled legs, he looks like a flea. Mandarich eats up his lifting partners. He had been through two dozen in college, none of whom could stand his pace, and he says of Smith, who has just now put a huge gob of snuff in his mouth and has been training daily with him for the last five months, "I'd rather lift with a little guy who's intense and crazy than with a dork who's my size and a puss."

They heave and grunt and curse and move maniacally from one rack of metal to another. The music blasts so loud that the clangs of the iron plates disappear into the rim shots and wails and monster chords of W. Axl's band. In the middle of a set Mandarich trembles and spits on the mirrored wall. "Die, fucker!" he yells as Smith's face nearly explodes like a squeezed tomato in the middle of a quivering military press.

Are these guys serious? This stuff doesn't have anything whatsoever to do with health, but everything to do with pain, risk, determination, and narcissism. "I'd rather do this than party," says Mandarich. "If I miss a day, I don't know what to do with myself."

Smith pants for air between sets. "Everybody's looking for the easy way out." he says. "But how many guys squat till they puke? We do."

They continue on, rack after rack, the little guy and the monstrosity.

"When you're big and intense, you're a motherfucker," states Mandarich, noting that it's spring break on campus, which is why the gym is so empty. "All the fat pigs are in Florida."

Finally, the two stop for a while and Mandarich explains the genesis of his compulsion. "I played at two seventy-five my sophomore year, and against Indiana I got run over by Van Waiters, their outside linebacker who's about six-four, two-fifty. He pushed me right back into Dave Yarema, our quarterback. That's the play. I said, 'That's enough.' I changed my life. I changed my priorities. I dedicated myself to the weight room. I quit getting hammered at night. I got rid of my girlfriend. She demanded too much. I said, 'I'm not getting embarrassed anymore!' I'm gonna go balls-out at whatever I do, or I'm not gonna do it. Lifting, football, music—balls-out. It doesn't matter, balls-out. The stereo in my truck, hey, that's no rinky-dink thing."

I knew this. I had ridden with him in his black Bronco, had seen the two-foot-high speakers that prevented anyone from sitting normally in the backseat, the 1,100-watt amplifier that took up the whole trunk, the high-tech equalizer and modulator under the steering column. He had turned on "The Bad Seamstress Blues" by Cinderella to show me how loud the system could get, and when the bass kicked in, it almost stopped my heart. We had picked up his new girlfriend, MSU student Amber Ligon, and gone to dinner at a Mexican restaurant, and he had continued his explanation of his priorities.

"We're moving to Los Angeles soon," he said. "That's where all the things I want are: Hollywood, the weather, the beaches, the bodybuilding scene, the music." He said that he was training out in Whittier with Rory Leidelmeyer, the reigning Mr. America, and that he hoped to become Mr. Universe when he was done playing ball. "I don't want to be a fat fuck like ninety percent of the NFL," he said between bites of an enchilada. "I want to be a football player who looks like a bodybuilder. For self-esteem. If I look like a slob, I'll play like one." He looked across the aisle at an out-of-shape couple with their whining children. "A lot of people are satisfied being smooth and fat and sitting at home with their kids. Not me." He looked at Amber. "If she gets fat, she's gone. She knows it. She knows when to talk, too, when not to say anything, when to just be quiet."

I turned to the young woman, a former violinist who was now heavily into bodybuilding herself and ready to follow her man to the coast. Was this true?

"Yes," she answered. "If it wasn't, I wouldn't be here."

So I visited Mandarich out in California, watched him move huge weights around in a dingy gym in Whittier with his buddy, Mr. America, watched him eat a two-pound steak for dinner, watched him shop at a grocery store and load up on enough food to keep a small-framed family alive for a month, observed the handcuffs around the gearshift of his truck and the framed portrait of Jesus over his bed, sat with him and Amber while we watched his hero, the 5′ 9″, 140-pound, heavily tattooed, long-haired, thoroughly wasted and bent W. Axl Rose on MTV, and then I wrote my story for *Sports Illustrated*. It was the end. I had seen the abyss. Rick Telander, over and out.

And the thing was, in a perverse way I *liked* Tony Mandarich. His lifestyle, his narcissism, his muscle mania, his killer instinct, tunnel vision, and money-hungry cockiness were all reasonable responses, I felt, to the pressures and hypocrisy of a sport that has gone too far. I would have wanted him on my team, I can tell you that. In the midst of a workout Mandarich had turned to me, sweating hard and grinning, and said, "Everybody's ass is up for grabs." Sweet anarchy.

The letters to the editor were brutal. Readers blasted Mandarich for being what he was and me for documenting it. What kind of role model was *SI* establishing here for youngsters throughout the free world? One letter, from a doctor at Massachusetts General Hospital in Boston, pretty much set the tone. "Dear S.I.," he wrote. "As a physician, I was horrified by Rick Telander's article on Tony Mandarich. He represents everything wrong with college athletics. An S.I. cover for a man who seeks to destroy and physically punish others, thrives on caffeine and a high-cholesterol diet, uses profanity in every sentence, and drops out of school will only lead to more recklessness by America's youth."

Well, Doc—I wanted to write back—*deal with it.* You people love college football, so you'd better love the crazy bastards who play it. As the limits of rationality and violence and profit-taking in college football get pushed farther into the stratosphere, this is what you get. Tony Mandarich is a great college football player. Make no mistake about it. None of his coaches, teammates, or lifting buddies has ever said a negative thing about him. And he destroys his opponents. He is what the system has wrought. He has the right attitude, the right body, everything. Does he use steroids? Who knows? Who cares? If a kid wants to be a great college lineman, he *should* be as weird as this guy. Weirdness works. What do you think they're playing out there, marbles?

And having said that, I must present my next point: Tony Mandarich has made me realize that *the game of football, as we know it, has become unplayable.* No one should have to perform against a creature like him. Certainly, no one pursuing knowledge through higher education should have to descend into such a shallow exploitation of the physical self. Weight

lifting, steroids, position specialization, and the
tudes that come with any or all of the above hav
game into a very dangerous freak show.

When Rutgers played Princeton in the first intercollegiate football game in 1869, the average size of the players was about 5′8″ and 150 pounds, which was greater than average for college students of the day. Of course, the players didn't wear helmets or pads or play football the way players do today, but they played a rough game, and if you had told them that someday behemoths ten inches taller than they and more than twice their weight would be lining up against one another, they probably would have snickered in your face. I guarantee you that if they had seen Tony Mandarich, live, across the line from them, they would have canceled the game of football for all time.

Sheer size, and the speed at which it moves, has made football a game that toys with the tolerance level of the human skeleton, sinews, muscles, and organs. Just think about Tony Mandarich falling on you, let alone delivering a blow at his full 4.65 speed. I read in the papers constantly about the increasing size of football players from the high school level on up. A 7′, 348-pound high school kid named Robert Jones signs a letter of intent with the University of New Hampshire. Willie "Porkchop" Hill, a 6′2″, 295-pound fullback signs to go to Michigan State. Three-hundred-pound linemen become the rule in the NFL. Coach Joe Walton of the New York Jets says he's pleased with the "athletic ability" of 6′7″, 380-pound offensive tackle Steve Collier. Mandarich someday, no doubt, will be considered a normally sculpted offensive tackle in the pros. And the irony of this is that with all the athlete conditioning and weight-training and improvement in the protective pads worn by players, we have cut down substantially on the most serious injuries in the sport. In 1905 there were twenty-three football deaths; in 1988 no college players were killed on the field. But instead of deaths, we now have minor injuries occurring on virtually every play, just from the impact of the players.

In his book *The Death of an American Game,* John Underwood wrote that an estimated one million high school players, 70,000 college players, and all NFL players suffer injuries each year. In last season's North Carolina high school all-star game, there were so many injuries that North Carolina State University alone lost four of its recruits to surgery. In 1986 the Denver Broncos had twenty-one players injured in a single exhibition game. There is now rather vague yet compelling evidence that playing football for many years shortens one's life substantially. Len Teeuws, a former NFL lineman and now an insurance actuary in Indianapolis and a trustee for the NFL Players Association Pension Program, recently studied 1,800 National Football League players who played at least five years between 1921 and 1959, and he found their average lifespan to be sixty-one years, well below the current national average of seventy-six years. "The actuarial science is not an exact science," Teeuws told me. "The league pooh-poohs these statistics. But I don't care what anybody says, this is what is happening. People don't realize how few of us old guys are left." Ron Mix, a Hall of Fame tackle who played for the San Diego Chargers in the 1960s and is now an attorney who handles workers' compensation and disability claims in California, has been compiling a death and disability study for the NFL Players Association. He has studied over 800 cases, and he estimates that the life expectancy for the average NFL player is fifty-five years and that the average player will be 50 to 64 percent disabled because of leg and back injuries. Nobody knows the causes of the mortality rate for sure, but Mix and others blame stress, steroids, brutal practices, collisions, painkillers, amphetamines, added weight, and concussions as just some of the reasons why players might die young.

Frank Woschitz, the director of public relations for the NFL Players Association, says that preliminary studies indicate that the game has become a lot more dangerous and psychologically troublesome since 1970. "That year seems to be an important year," says Woschitz, pointing out the increased stress on players, due to greater rewards and pressure to win, the influx of artificial turf, and the increase in player size and strength since then. "And the thing people forget is that pro players didn't just hatch at age twenty-two," says Woschitz. "NFL players have already been through four years of high school ball and four years of college ball, where the same serious injuries and beatings are occurring. NFL players are survivors. Many players are already too injured to continue past college." A recent study done by two Ball State University professors and a counseling psychologist shows that two-thirds of all NFL players since 1970 are left with a permanent injury when they retire. Forty percent of the former players feel anger or resentment toward the game for those injuries, and two-thirds admit to experiencing emotional problems after leaving the game, problems they largely attribute to their careers in football.

It's a great sport to be promoting on college campuses, isn't it?

Not long ago I talked with Dick Kazmaier, the former Princeton tailback and 1951 Heisman Trophy winner, and he noted how much the players had changed since he played. "I was five-eleven, one hundred seventy pounds and I looked not much different than most people," he said. "I never lifted weights. Even the biggest linemen weren't over two hundred ten pounds. I never had any injuries, either, except a sprained ankle and a broken nose. Of course, we didn't have face masks. The biggest difference, besides size, was the way players used to tackle. They used their shoulders and the side-body technique."

Now, of course, you plant your helmet on the ballcarrier's numbers and try to drive your body through the man. While at Baylor, middle linebacker Mike Singletary tackled opponents so hard that he broke sixteen helmets in four years. Do you know how hard it is to break a football helmet? Have you ever tried to shatter the hull of a motorboat with your fist? With your skull? You could take a helmet in your hand, hold it by the face mask, and swing it as hard as you could at an oak tree and you won't break it. If you got a really sturdy helmet, you could toss it up in the air like a baseball, rear back, and wallop it with 42-ounce Louisville Slugger and do it no damage. Scary things happen out on the football field these days simply from the vector forces and torques of huge men moving too fast. In the 1989 Super Bowl, Cincinnati Bengals noseguard Tim Krumrie drove to make an open-field tackle, and his own momentum snapped his left leg in half as though it were a willow branch. Of course, *Sports Illustrated* photographers were on the spot, and the ensuing stop-action photo in the Super Bowl issue, showing Krumrie's foot going one way and his leg the other, made me drop the magazine, fall back in my chair, and gag. Krumrie, as you might suspect, is a devoted weight lifter and he's working out right now, pumping up so he can get back into the game.

The trouble with weight lifting is that it rapidly goes beyond any basic strengthening or conditioning aspects that might benefit players in overall safety, and heads straight into compulsion and the use of the newfound muscles as weapons in and of themselves. For almost a century weight lifting was considered to be of no benefit to football players. The old saw was that it would make you inflexible and awkward and, basically, muscle-bound. I wrote about Dick Butkus awhile back and he told me that he probably could have extended his injury-plagued career if he had lifted weights, but that he did some bench presses once as a kid and the bar slipped and broke his wrist and that was enough for him.

The real weight-lifting stampede didn't begin until the late 1960s, when college teams began to understand the benefits of powerlifting for a contact sport like football and started to make strength conditioning part of their mandatory off-season work-outs. Schools such as Nebraska, which got into weight training hard and early, reaped the benefits of having stronger and more dominating players at the line of scrimmage than most of their opponents. When the Nebraska team arrived by plane in Miami for the 1989 Orange Bowl, it was followed shortly by a tractor trailer loaded down with weight-training equipment, which was then set up under the stadium at the team's practice field so the Huskers' precious muscles wouldn't atrophy in the days before the contest. Indeed, current Cornhuskers pump iron in Lincoln in a gigantic weightroom so sacred that red velvet ropes separate visitors from such relics as THE ORIGINAL HUSKER DUMBBELLS and THE ORIGINAL HUSKER PREACHER CURL PLATFORM (both of which, according to the plaques, are CIRCA 1967). All sports teams at Nebraska, even the women's volleyball team, worship at the strength shrine; the volleyballers' latest poster shows them posed in the weightroom under the fearsome headline: "Pound for Pound." When I stood in front of the red ropes recently, I myself was nearly overcome with the desire to charge out into the midst of the athletes and start madly hoisting away to get huge.

The downside to weight lifting is that it becomes an end in itself, and the football players who lift, which is everybody these days, quite often become entranced by the process itself. They see their muscles grow and start to sense a control over themselves that they never knew before. The pain of lifting is a natural adjunct to the pain of the game itself. The muscle-building process is particularly seductive for football players since they are already uncertain of their masculinity and can easily come to equate muscle mass with machismo, and machismo with self-worth. Serious, hard-core competitive body builders (and now some football players) are, in my opinion, so neurotically compulsive that their devotion to their sport has all the earmarks of an addiction. In fact, I feel that serious iron pumping is in many ways the male equivalent of anorexia nervosa; the lifters only feel in control of their bodies and themselves when their muscles are engorged with blood and screaming for mercy. Consider this description of the disease from the *American Psychiatric Association: Diagnostic and Statistical Manual of Mental Disorders,* the reference bible for clinical psychiatrists and psychologists, with my word substitutions in parentheses to indicate the differences between anorexia and muscle addiction: "The essential features of this disorder are: refusal to maintain body weight over (under) a minimal (maximal) normal weight for age and height; intense fear of gaining (losing) weight or becoming fat (losing muscle mass), even though underweight (well-built); a distorted body image. . . .

"The disturbance in body image is manifested by the way in which the person's body weight, size, or shape is experienced. People with this disorder say they 'feel fat' ('feel skinny'), or that parts of their body are 'fat' ('skinny'), when they are obviously underweight (well-muscled) or even emaciated (muscle-bound). They are preoccupied with their body size and usually dissatisfied with some feature of their physical appearance.

"The weight loss (muscle gain) is usually accomplished by a reduction (increase) in total food intake, often with extensive exercising. Frequently there is self-induced vomiting (excessive eating) or use of laxatives or diuretics (food supplements or steroids)."

I watched Mandarich and his lifting pals work out several times, and quite frankly, the physique of his 6′1″, 275-pound California lifting buddy, Rory Leidelmeyer, Mr. America, gave me the creeps. He was shaved and tanned, as he had to be, I guess, but he was also sporting these gratuitously swollen things, these muscles, that had no function whatsoever except as props to be put on display. I doubt that he could have swung a golf club, shot a free throw, or run more than a few hundred yards without seizing up like a giant clam. Leidelmeyer told me that when he worked a single muscle group hard—real, real hard—that bundle of fibers sometimes would swell up like a purple balloon, and in the case of his overdeveloped triceps sometimes hang over his elbow like a sack.

Am I the only person who finds that weird? I think not. *Muscle & Fitness* magazine, the Joe Weider–produced bodybuilding bible, talks routinely about silicone implants for men whose calves aren't developed enough and for women whose breasts have all but disappeared through intensive training. If you ask me, the whole bodybuilding subculture is like a freak show at the circus.

And another bad part of the weightlifting-bodybuilding-football connection is that steroid use goes along with it very nicely. Properly called *androgenic anabolic steroids:* androgenic, meaning male-sex-hormone-like; anabolic, meaning material that the body uses to build itself; and steroid, referring to the class of drugs these are, sterols. These drugs are to football players, particularly the ones who crave size and muscle, as booze is to alcoholics. Basically, the steroids used by athletes to increase their size and strength and, occasionally, endurance are all derivatives of the male sex hormone, testosterone. Testosterone is naturally secreted by the male testes, and it does such things as stimulate the growth of certain organs, promote sexual characteristics at puberty (larynx enlargement, vocal-cord thickening, penis enlargement, body-hair growth, oil-gland secretion, and muscle-mass increase, among other things), as well as affect one's libido and aggressiveness. It is, as they say, the thing that makes a bull a bull.

Football players take steroids in pill form or inject them in solution into fatty tissue, usually their buttocks or legs, where the hormones are slowly dispersed to the bloodstream. What the steroids do for the players is enhance muscle growth and the ability of the athlete to train harder and recover more quickly from the duress of training. Lifting weights, after all, is nothing more than the systematic tearing down of one's muscle tissue so that the damaged fibers will then rebuild themselves into sturdier and larger packets. Steroid use gets the muscles to repair themselves faster than normal.

The problem with steroid use—and it's worthwhile noting

here that steroids are *never* prescribed by ethical, competent doctors for use by athletes or any other healthy persons—is that it tinkers with the essential equilibrium of the body. As Dr. Bob Goldman, one of the world's best-known authorities on steroid abuse, writes in his book on athletic drug usage, *The "E" Factor,* "There is a carefully calibrated balance of hormones in the body that serves as an internal protective system. If this system is disturbed, problems may arise." Indeed. Goldman lists the problems steroids can cause: acne, baldness, water retention, atrophied testes, liver cancer, tumor production, prostate cancer, development of female breast tissue in males (in women, the development of facial hair, the deepening of the voice, and enlargement of the clitoris), premature closing of growth plates in bones, kidney disease, high blood pressure, and heart disease.

And there are the psychological problems the drugs promote: manic behavior, depression, paranoia, visual and auditory hallucinations, grandiose delusions. The steroids make their users edgy and aggressive, often unable to sleep well, and filled with a sense that they are big and bad and very nearly invincible. Tommy Chaikin has told me about the bar fights he got into during the depths of his steroid abuse because he felt so wound up and fierce—a brawl with a Marine in which he almost killed the Marine after the man had hit him under the chin and clipped off part of his tongue; another fight in which he was stabbed under the right arm with a twelve-inch deer knife and nearly bled to death. A buddy of his, also on steroids, routinely headbutted the windshields of parked cars until the glass shattered. The steroid-using players on that South Carolina team—and Tommy estimates that at one point over forty of his teammates had tried or were using steroids—often acted bizarrely and antisocially, as do football players on many teams.

Particularly horrifying, to me at least, were the descriptions of the "shooting parties" Tommy and his buddies would hold in their athletic dorm rooms. "It became a big social thing,"

Tommy told me. "Seven or eight of us heavy users would get together in a dorm room and start shooting each other up. Guys would show up with their bottles, and there'd be a lot of chatter: I shoot you, you shoot me. We all enjoyed it. I had boxes of syringes that I got from certain pharmacies in Columbia for twenty bucks a hundred. We never used the same needle twice, I can tell you that. We tried to be careful how we injected each other, too, but sometimes you'd hit the sciatic nerve or something, and the guy's legs would buckle. I mean, none of us were doctors or anything. But we were needle happy. We would have injected ourselves with anything if we thought it would make us big.

"A lot of times, if we were really getting bigger, we'd increase our dosage to gain bulk even faster—just fill the syringe to the end. We'd occasionally read the paperwork that came with the bottles, trying to figure out what a dosage should be for someone with anemia or a guy whose body can't produce enough testosterone, which is what the stuff is usually used for. Then we'd take two, three, four, ten, twenty times that amount. Sometimes we'd take our needles and pull half a cc from one bottle and half from another, just mix them up. The more the better."

It was crazy, absolutely insane, what Tommy Chaikin was doing. And he knew it, but it didn't matter. Such was the pull of the sport on his fragile, postadolescent ego that even when he knew the drugs were making him mentally ill, he could not stop taking them—because they were making him better at the game. His aggression level was so high that at one point he got into an argument with the team trainer over something of no importance, then went to his locker and put his hand through the metal mesh and ripped the door off its hinges. "I was benching close to five hundred pounds, squatting more than six hundred," Tommy told me. "I could do thirty one-armed presses with a hundred-pound dumbbell. I weighed about two sixty and I looked like a steroid user, all swollen and tight. [He now weighs about 210 and looks like a muscular but normal human being.] I was taking all kinds of steroids, including Equipoise, a horse steroid designed to make thoroughbreds leaner and more muscular. After I ruined my locker, I went back to the dorm and took a baseball bat and demolished my refrigerator, smashed it to pieces, and then ripped the phone off the wall. At practice one day I got into a fight with Shed Diggs, a linebacker, because he cut in front of me in line for a drill. I threw him down, pulled his helmet up far enough so I could get my fist in there, and smashed him in the eye. As he got up, bleeding and humiliated, I felt sympathy for him. But then the steroids kicked in and I said to myself, 'All right! You're a tough guy!' ''

Tommy recognized that he was turning into a sick, violent animal, but he didn't feel he could stop taking steroids without losing his position on the South Carolina team or his self-esteem. ''My sense of self-worth was completely tied up in the game,'' he says. The bottom line for Tommy, as it is for other players, is that the steroids made him big, strong, and aggressive, which is just what you want for the game. It is just what coaches want, too. Indeed, one of the most distressing aspects of Tommy's case is that at least one of his coaches seemed to know what Tommy was doing to himself and encouraged it.

How prevalent is steroid usage in football? Nobody knows for sure, but various studies and personal estimates by players make it seem quite common. In May, Atlanta Falcon guard Bill Fralic told a Senate Judiciary Committee hearing on the dangers of steroids that he estimates that ''probably about seventy-five percent'' of NFL linemen, linebackers, and tight ends use the drugs. Former NFL guard Steve Courson, thirty-three, who believes that his own previous heavy steroid use is responsible for causing the coronary problems that have now forced him to seek a heart transplant, testified that he thinks that half the players at line-of-scrimmage positions in the NFL take steroids. Several University of Miami players told a *Sports Illustrated* reporter that as many as two-thirds of the players from the 1987

Fiesta Bowl team used steroids. In the spring of 1987, former Hurricanes' equipment manager Marty Daly said, "You'd come in and find syringes in the corner of the locker room," and Miami players themselves admitted using steroids up to six weeks before the Fiesta Bowl, but avoided detection by switching from oil-based to water-based steroids.

The July 1988 issue of *The Physician and Sportsmedicine* estimates that the number of steroid-abusing males in America, even from "conservative extrapolations," is in the hundreds of thousands. And most of those users, it appears, are young. An article published in the 1988 year-end issue of the *Journal of the American Medical Association* found that 6.6 percent of male high school seniors—as many as a half-million nationwide—use or have used steroids. "We're not talking about casual use of anabolic steroids," says the primary author of the study, William E. Buckley, an assistant professor of health and education at Penn State. The young athletes are "stacking the drugs [taking more than one type simultaneously for the potluck muscle-building effect], and thirty percent are using needles," says Buckley. "That's fairly hard-core behavior."

Yes, it is. In fact, it's mind-boggling. Wasn't that always part of the horror we felt over the behavior of smack junkies, that the addicts could so casually invade their own bodies with needles squirting God knows what into their veins? And to think of 150,000 or so high school kids shooting up so they can get bigger—it chills one to the bone.

Where did steroids come from anyway? According to a recent article in the medical journal *Hippocrates*, the use of steroids for athletic purposes started as far back as 1889 when Charles-Edouard Brown-Sequard, a seventy-two-year-old French physician living in England, decided to experiment on himself to see if he could cure his chronic fatigue and exhaustion. He injected himself with the liquid crushed from the testicles of a young dog and rapidly began to feel rejuvenated. Within days he found he could again dash up and down stairs. "The feebleness of old men is in part due to the diminution of the function of the testicles,'' he wrote. Within a year doctors worldwide were injecting patients with ''testicular fluid,'' heralding it as a cure for everything from old age to cancer, epilepsy, cholera, and leprosy. We didn't hear too much about steroids after that until the 1950s, when the athletes from certain Eastern Bloc countries began using steroids to make extraordinary muscle gains to aid them in their sports. At an international weight-lifting championship, Dr. John Ziegler, the American team physician, learned from the Russian team doctor that the Soviets were experimenting with male hormones as an aid to building strength. Ziegler came back to the United States and with the help of a pharmaceutical company developed the granddaddy of American sports steroid pills, Dianabol, so common among certain sports groups that today it is often referred to as ''dirt.'' Ziegler started various weight lifters on low doses of the drug in the 1960s but was soon dismayed to find that the athletes liked the drug so much that they would take much more than was prescribed, heedless of the physical dangers.

In *The ''E'' Factor,* Goldman writes: ''It had been Dr. Ziegler's intention to help preserve our winning ways in sports, but it turned into a nightmare for him. John Ziegler was one of the finest men I have ever known. I had the honor of studying under him for eight years. He died in November 1983, several days before his sixtieth birthday. The last time we spoke he told me he wished he could wipe that whole chapter from his life. Since then the steroid epidemic has spread through the entire sports world.''

Like many of the recreational drugs that first became widely used in the turbulent 1960s and early '70s, steroids were initially considered to be relatively benign and thus were able to gain a foothold in the sports world they might otherwise not have. One need only look back a few years to some of the statements made by people in authority regarding the safety of cocaine to realize how wrong we can be in our assessment of newly popular drugs. In 1974, Dr. Peter Bourne, who would later become President Jimmy Carter's drug adviser, called cocaine "probably the most benign of illicit drugs." And as late as 1977, *Newsweek* wrote this virtual paean to coke: "Among hostesses in the smart sets of Los Angeles and New York, a little cocaine, like Dom Pérignon and Beluga caviar, is now de rigueur at dinners. Some partygoers pass it around along with the canapés on silver trays. . . . Cocaine is a stimulant—an 'up'—and produces none of the blurred perception or memory lapse that often accompanies the use of marijuana. The user experiences a feeling of potency, of confidence, of energy."

Likewise, there have been a lot of statements by people in positions of authority in the international sports world claiming that steroids are not such bad things. "Why do we make such a drama out of this?" asks Dr. Heinz Liesen, a physician for the West German national soccer team. "If a body cannot regenerate itself by producing a sufficient amount of hormone, then it is certainly appropriate to help it out, just as one would give it vitamin C, B_1 or B_2 or stimulate its immune system, so that it can recuperate rather than remain sick." In a paper on the future of scientific sport presented to The American Academy of Physical Education and The American Alliance for Health, Physical Education, Recreation and Dance at those organizations' 1987 national convention, professor John Hoberman of the University of Texas quoted a Swedish strength coach as saying in 1984, "Our ethical and moral rules have maintained that one must not administer anything to the body. But I view the hormonal substances as a progressive development comparable to the use of fiberglass poles by vaulters." That kind of reasoning trickles down to affect, at least subliminally, anyone who competes in big-time sport. As Hoberman stated in his article:

> As we have already seen, the use of manipulative technologies is poisoning relationships throughout the world of high-performance sport. Dr. Wildor Hollmann, head of the Institute for

> Sport Medicine and Circulatory Research in Cologne and the current president of the International Federation for Sport Medicine, stated in 1984: "No one trusts anyone anymore. Every athlete asks himself what the other one crouching next to him in the starting blocks is doing, what kinds of things he has been taking in the course of his training in order to win. And if the athlete who asks himself this stands there completely clean and loses, then he may later call himself a fool for having behaved in this way." What is more, this is a permanent state of affairs. "Never again," Dr. Hollmann stated in 1985, "not even in the remote future, will we see a high-performance sport without doping problems."

That is an undoubtedly true, if unfortunate, statement about modern sports competition. But it brings up the ethical dilemma involved in preparation for any big-time sport, football or otherwise. How far does one go to get that edge, to be the best athlete possible, and yet still remain an ethical human being? Lying is so prevalent in sports now, particularly when it comes to admitting drug use, that to trust someone regarding his own drug usage is to be, as the doctor says, a fool. Was Tony Mandarich telling me the truth when he said he'd never used steroids? I don't know. And I'm only willing to do so much to find out. I don't want to be a private investigator or walk around with a urinalysis kit and say, "Here, pal, let's have a sample."

It will be a long time before I trust any bodybuilders or weight-lifting muscle freaks, I can tell you that. When I was writing about Benji Ramirez, the high school kid on steroids whose heart exploded in Ashtabula, I stopped in at a supermarket in that Ohio town to pick up a copy of *Muscle & Fitness*. Benji had died in November on the practice field at Ashtabula High, and after the autopsy, Ashtabula County coroner Robert Malinowski listed steroid use as a contributing factor in the seventeen-year-old's death, the first time the drugs had ever legally been linked to an athlete's death in the United States. Benji's friends had told me that *M&F* was one of Benji's favorite magazines, that he loved to gaze at photos of beefcakes like Lee Haney and Bob Paris and imagine what it would be like to be ripped and shredded just like them.

I saw a large picture of "Naturally Trained World Champion" Louis Freitas in the magazine and paused to read the copy beside it. "It feels great being natural," Freitas said. "I'm healthy and fit, and the body I'm building is 100% beef—nothing artificial added! Because my body is the result of intense training and good nutrition, I'm in peak condition year-round. Training and competing the natural way is more challenging. But I'm proof that a natural bodybuilder can be a big winner—if you eat right, train hard, and follow Joe Weider's wise advice. . . ." Basically, that advice had to do with lifting hard and eating properly and taking some silly Joe Weider "free-form branched-chain amino acid" garbage that would give you "nutritional confidence" and possibly gigantic biceps just like Freitas. Okay, that's cool, I thought. Spend a little money on some vitamins and eat them instead of steroids and nobody gets hurt. It's just a harmless scam, and what the heck, I remember all the junk I ate as a kid trying to get bigger—Meritene, I think some of the stuff was called, and Tiger Milk and something that looked like granulated plaster that I mixed with two eggs, milk, a banana, ice cream, and about a pint of chocolate syrup and drank every night before bedtime—and it all made me feel like I was doing something constructive and none of it killed me.

But then, no more than a few days after I left Ashtabula, I read that ex–Mr. Universe Freitas had been busted by U.S. Customs agents on charges of conspiracy and possession of illegal anabolic steroids with intent to distribute. He got nailed in Columbus, where he had arrived to attend the Arnold Schwarzenegger Classic bodybuilding contest. Columbus isn't too far from Ashtabula, and I wondered if Benji, were he alive, would have attended the contest himself, just to gape, and whether he would have met the "naturally trained" Freitas somewhere in the crowd, had Freitas not gotten pinched earlier, and maybe bought some "real" muscle-building juice from the phony son of a bitch.

I'm assuming virtually all pro wrestling contestants are on steroids, because they look like it and that's what I've heard from inside sources. Also, in my opinion, any elite-level track weight man is guilty of steroid use unless he can prove himself innocent. Last year, the news that there would be drug testing at a big Los Angeles track meet forced promoter Al Franken to cancel the shot put after all the top athletes in that event withdrew. And probably most elite track and field athletes in any event are users of some banned substance. In 1988 sprinter Gwen Torrence described U.S. track and field as "one of the biggest drug rings you can imagine," and she was backed up by a number of other top U.S. track athletes, including sprinter Evelyn Ashford and hurdler Roger Kingdom. Carl Lewis has often gotten on the soap box to lash out at the drug users in track and field. The Toronto-based Charles Dubin Inquiry into drug usage by Canadian track and field athletes has shown that the athletes in that country are mired in a cesspool of steroid abuse as well. Canadian weight lifter Denis Garon told the panel that he took steroids because his competitors from the rest of the world were taking them. It was a simple equation. "I need drugs to win medals," he testified. "Canada wants to win medals."

Steve Courson gives us the football player's version of the same lament: "What's a nosetackle supposed to do when he knows his coach expects him to weigh two hundred ninety-five pounds and bench-press six hundred pounds?" There is an essential dilemma here, for the effects of steroids can, as we have mentioned, produce several of the qualities that are desired by football coaches everywhere. As Bill Fralic says, "The system rewards you for being a good football player, no matter what the means are to the end."

Football's emphasis on contact makes the "everybody's doing it'' argument even more compelling. If a shot-putter's opponents are all taking steroids and he's not, he'll probably be beaten; if the same is true for a football lineman, he'll probably be beaten up, and badly. It's not just competition for a job that drives a football player to bulk up artificially; it's the fear that his opponents might have some weapons in their arsenal that he's lacking. It's easy for the player to persuade himself that he needs that edge not just to excel, but to be able to walk off the field in one piece.

When sprint world-record-holder Ben Johnson was nailed for using steroids at the 1988 Olympics and was subsequently stripped of his gold medal in the 100-meter dash, it pointed out to the world how deeply rooted steroid use is in the realm of sport, and perhaps, how effective. Dr. Mario Astaphan, the physician who prescribed and administered the steroids to Johnson, told the Dubin Inquiry that the working axiom in big-time sport is, ''If you don't take it, you won't make it.'' Even conceding that point to Astaphan, who, in this writer's opinion, is one of the most unethical people ever to take the Hippocratic oath, what of the health risks to the athletes themselves? Dr. Goldman has an intriguing answer to that question. A few years ago he performed a survey in which he asked 198 world-class athletes the following question: ''If I had a magic drug that was so fantastic if you took it once you would win every competition you entered, from the Olympic decathlon to Mr. Universe, for the next five years, but it had one minor drawback—it would kill you five years after you took it—would you still take the drug?'' Of those asked, 103 (52 percent) said they would. It can be argued, Goldman noted after the survey, that it was only because the athletes knew there was no such magic medicine that they claimed they would take it despite the certain death sentence. ''But evidence suggests that athletes will take anything, or do anything to their bodies, to win,'' Goldman wrote, ''even with no real assurance of winning.''

So what we're left with to prevent steroid abuse by those who feel no ethical constraints against taking the drugs is drug testing. And what a mess that whole procedure is. The three biggest problems with drug testing are: one, the expense—a single comprehensive test to detect performance-enhancing and recreational drugs can cost more than a hundred dollars per sample, making frequent testing or testing of large groups, such as all high school football players, prohibitively costly; two, the invasion of privacy of the tests that makes them legally and morally suspect, since they seem to disregard the Fourth Amendment's prohibition on unreasonable searches as well as any reasonable person's desire not to be humiliated; and three, they are not infallible or sensitive to new performance-enhancing drugs or masking agents designed to beat the tests. As Dr. Astaphan boasted to the Canadian committee, "I know sufficient about anabolic steroids and the way to beat any test. . . . There are anabolic steroids completely undetectable by the International Olympic Committee."

Ben Johnson himself was just unlucky; reports have stated that he needed perhaps only forty-eight hours more to metabolize the traces of the steroid that was found in his urine. Johnson told the Dubin Inquiry that he had taken steroids since 1981, which left the world to ponder how the sprinter had been able to pass nineteen drug tests in the years leading up to the 1988 Olympics. Clearly, Astaphan was a man of his word; the doctor did know how to beat the tests. As Dr. Charles Yesalis III, a professor of Health and Human Development at Penn State, notes, "Steroids are training drugs. They do not need to be present in the body at the time of competition to give the user a competitive edge." So the tests become problematic; passing one may not mean an athlete is off drugs or hasn't used them in the recent past, but it nevertheless gives him the right to claim to be drug-free.

I wonder if we need this kind of briar-patch controversy in college sports. I remember covering the 1988 NCAA basketball East Regional, and waiting outside the drug-testing station after

Duke beat Rhode Island in a 73–72 thriller. I wanted to talk to Danny Ferry or one of his buddies. I waited and waited and occasionally I would look into the room and see the Duke starters silently walking around, still in their game uniforms, drinking water or Coca-Cola or Gatorade, with personal monitors dogging their every step. Each monitor was a guy who would stay glued to a player until that man physically peed in a bottle, right there in front of the monitor's own two eyes. I waited over a half-hour for one of the players to come out, then gave up and talked to some of the scrubs, thinking how ridiculous and embarrassing the whole procedure was. Georgetown coach John Thompson said something about drug testing during the season that makes sense to me. "Don't make me a scapegoat for drug testing," he said. "Don't put that monkey on my back. I ain't a cop. If you want to do drug testing, let the police department do it, and when you catch them put 'em in jail. But don't tell me to test for drugs. That is not my job."

Drugs are certainly a Pandora's box of evil for both sport and society, and if you recall the Pandora mythology, you'll remember that once the evils flew out of the fair maiden's sealed vessel, there was no getting them back into it. Drugs are here to stay. And in truth, athletes have been searching for that drug-induced edge since the beginning of competition. It's interesting to note that the winner of the 1904 Olympic marathon in St. Louis, Thomas Hicks of Cambridge, Massachusetts, admitted after the race that he had used "stimulants," including brandy and strychnine, to spur himself on. (It's even more interesting to note that Hicks was declared the winner only after the first finisher, Fred Lorz of New York, admitted he covered 11 of the 26.2 miles in an automobile.)

And who knows what the next drug of favor will be for football players? Already I'm hearing more and more about athletes who are taking HGH, human growth hormone, to increase their size. HGH can now be synthetically produced, but some of it still comes from its initial source, the pituitary glands of cadavers. Athletes who would use that stuff would almost certainly use Goldman's mythical elixir regardless of the consequences. As past Olympic javelin thrower Kate Schmidt says, "The thought that we are going to get rid of drugs in sports is highly amusing."

Colleges don't need to be associated with this craziness.

The one part of football that separates it from all other sports is tackling. Tackling is the primitive, essential element that both thrills and terrifies the game's participants and viewers. I know the Chicago Bears' Mike Singletary fairly well, and I wrote a feature on him before Chicago played in Super Bowl XX in 1986. Singletary, several times the NFL's Defensive Player of the Year, began describing some of his helmet-busting, guided-missile tackles in a near-rapturous tone that sprang from his Zen-like immersion in the chaos of the game. One brutal hit on running back Eric Dickerson stuck out in his mind.

"I don't feel pain from a hit like that," he said. "What I feel is joy. Joy for the tackle. Joy for myself. Joy for the other man. You understand me; I understand you. It's football, it's middle-linebacking. It's just . . . good for everybody."

The clarity and reward for a hit like that are deeply rooted in the dark essence of the game. But the type of tackling we see now—"I try to visualize my head all the way through the man," says Singletary, "my whole body through him"—is relatively new and different from the way tackling was done in the past, and the main reason is the advent a couple of decades ago of the hard-shell, air- and water-filled helmet with the increasingly large and protective face mask. Modern-day helmets allow face-first tackles, burying "your nose on his numbers" as the coaches say, so that the helmet is now less a protective device than a weapon, a rock-hard spear point that is almost always the first part of a defensive player's uniform to touch the ballcarrier. Don Cooper, the team physician at Oklahoma State, calls the helmet "the damnedest, meanest tool on the face of the earth."

And if you've ever been hit by one, with someone else's head inside it, moving at a high rate of speed, you know what the doctor means.

I was reading former Oakland Raider and Buffalo Bills wide receiver Bob Chandler's book, *Violent Sundays,* a few years ago when I came to a part that grabbed my attention. I remembered covering Chandler when he played for Southern Cal and our teams met in the Coliseum in Los Angeles. "My junior year, we played Northwestern in our opening game," he wrote. "I went down to catch a low ball, and the halfback speared me in my lower back. I wasn't sure what was damaged, but I couldn't feel my right leg, which scared the hell out of me. I hobbled off the field. Later, back at my apartment, I was in such agony that by the middle of the night my roommate Gerry Mullins literally had to pick me up, carry me to his car, and take me to the hospital. After a battery of X rays, [Coach] John McKay came in and said matter-of-factly, 'Looks like you broke your back.' "

Chandler said he was hit by a "halfback," which meant it had to have been either Jack Dustin or I who had done the damage, since we were the two cornerbacks who played for Northwestern that night. I remembered Chandler as a shifty, glue-fingered little white guy, but my biggest concern that game had been trying to stay with 6′3″, lightning-bolt split end Sam Dickerson. I didn't remember hitting anybody particularly hard or making much of an impact on the game in any way, but the fact was, I might have broken an opponent's back with my helmet and not even realized I had done so. I asked Dustin, who is now a physician, if he remembered hitting Chandler in the back. He said he couldn't recall.

I finally ran into Chandler himself in the press box at an NFL game. Chandler was working as a sportscaster for a TV station in L.A., and he looked about the same as I remembered him from college. I asked him if it could have been I who had broken his back years ago, if he remembered the player's number. He said he didn't remember the number, but for some reason, he didn't think I was the man. Why, he couldn't say. Probably, it was because I just looked too harmless standing there with my notebook in my back pocket and press ID hanging from a shirt button. Still, the incident haunts me. The thought that any player could do such damage to an opponent with his helmet and not even know it is an indictment of some fundamental part of the game.

A friend of mine, sportswriter Don Pierson, who covers the NFL for the *Chicago Tribune,* recently loaned me a notebook of his from his undergrad days at Ohio State. The notebook is from a credited course Pierson took in 1966 called The Coaching of Football, taught by one Woodrow Wilson Hayes, and open to all students at the university. The maintaining of a notebook was the main work for the course, and at the back of Pierson's notebook is written in red ink: " 'A' Excellent! W.W.H." The reason Pierson wanted me to take a look at the notes was to see the section on tackling. Hayes called in his right-hand man to class that day, defensive coordinator Lou McCullough, and let him explain the proper way to stick an opponent. McCullough, who would later become the athletic director at Iowa State, had a Southern drawl, Pierson informed me, and I needed to keep that in mind as I read the text. Herewith:

> We don't like to see a kid making a tackle like he is trying to *hug* the man down. We want to give him cancer of the breast by knocking his titty off. We want to knock his anus up through his *haid.*

That's verbatim, and I still howl every time I read it. But I think you can see why the helmet now comes with a product liability sticker on it, one that must remain on the helmet during play, as if players might stop to casually peruse the warning during lulls in the action. The label reads, "Do not use this Helmet to butt, ram or spear an opposing player. This is in violation of the football rules and such use can result in severe head or neck injuries, paralysis or death to you and possible injury to your opponent. No helmet can prevent all head or neck injuries a player might receive while participating in football.''

In other words, the way coaches teach their players to tackle, face-first, may be damaging to their health. But that's how the game is played—if such a harmless word as ''play'' can be applied to this increasingly violent spectacle.

Worse, some players feel invincible once they strap on their headgear, at least partly because the helmets themselves make the players feel like Kralite-hulled gladiators. Back in November 1987, I read something in the newspaper that haunted me as I went about covering college football. A boy named Doug Mansfield, a 5′10″, 165-pound senior noseguard at Humboldt High School in Tennessee, had run headfirst into a brick wall in frustration after a close loss to Lexington High and was now paralyzed from the neck down. The wire service report stated that moments after the game ended, the youth had run in full football gear directly into the wall outside the dressing room. The blow broke his neck and severed his spinal cord and left him in critical condition. ''The doctors said there is nothing we can do, that he won't ever get any better,'' his mother, Susan Mansfield, was quoted as saying. ''We're just praying and waiting it out.''

I thought about the incident so much as the months went by, wondered what it was that had forced such a horrible fate on the football player, that a year and a half after the accident I decided to track down young Mansfield himself. I heard from Billy Reed, an *SI* writer in Kentucky, that Mansfield had been an ''A'' student and apparently had been offered an academic scholarship to Mississippi State or some other large southern school before the tragedy.

I spoke with Jim Potee, the principal and athletic director at Humboldt High. ''I was within twenty-five to thirty yards of him when it happened,'' said Potee. ''He was going up the hill where the dressing room is, and he had his helmet in his hand. He put in on, buckled both chin straps, lowered his head, and ran straight into the wall. That was the last time he moved.''

The only question I could ask was, why?

''He was frustrated. It was the first round of the state playoffs, and we had the game won but gave it away when we had a touchdown called back and then fumbled to let them score. We lost, fourteen to thirteen. He had nothing to do with the loss, but he was a fierce competitor. What he had, he gave you. He was a great person, too—a fine student and a great artist. We still use some of his paintings in our yearbook.''

I asked the principal if he thought the boy had been trying to hurt himself.

''Oh, no, it was not intentional,'' Potee answered. ''He had no concept of the danger. It was like if you would kick a car tire or hit a door with your fist in anger. In that uniform and helmet you think you're protected against all elements.''

I remembered the old football cliché that tells players that with enough heart and guts a kid can run right through a brick wall. Coaches love to expound on that. I wondered if that myth had played a role in Doug Mansfield's tragedy.

I asked Potee how the boy was doing now, if there was any hope for recovery.

''Oh,'' said the man. ''You didn't know. He's dead. He died at the spinal injury center in Atlanta three months after the game.''

Pete Gent once wrote, ''Psychotic episodes are a daily occurrence in a business where the operative phrase is, 'Stick your head in there.' '' And he is right. The use of the head—the thinking center, the housing (scientists and philosophers now suspect) for the soul, the very thing that contains that which separates us from beasts—as the primary weapon in football tends to warp logic and reward people on the fringes of sanity. It's not enough to say that the sport rewards aggressiveness. The best players often are those who are the most reckless with their own well-being, the most willing to do crazy, dangerous things with their own bodies and, consequently, to other people's bodies. "Nobody will know what I'm talking about unless they strap on a helmet and run forty yards downfield and hit a guy who doesn't see you coming," says Phoenix Cardinals special-teams player Ron Wolfley, on the joys of football. "Now that's comedy to me." Is anybody laughing?

I think about the profile I had to do for *SI* on Detroit Lions linebacker Jimmy Williams two years ago. Williams can be almost rabid on the field, fighting and swearing like a man possessed, though off the field he is quiet and retiring, a Sunday school teacher at a Baptist church in Pontiac, Michigan, among other things. Of course, such Jekyll and Hyde behavior is pretty normal for high-level football players. But I asked Williams specifically if he liked hurting people on the field. "If it's between getting an interception and putting a hit on the receiver," he said, "I'll always hit the receiver. I like to hit a man and hear that . . ."

He smiled warily, afraid that maybe he had revealed too much.

Hear what, I asked.

"Hear that little. . ."

Yes?

He thought a moment. His smile grew. "That little moan."

When Auburn linebacker Aundray Bruce, the first player taken in the 1988 NFL draft, was in college, he sometimes worked himself into such a frenzy of malevolence at the line of scrimmage that tears would stream down his face. There has been at least one study done that shows that in certain adolescent boys the line between aggression or violence and sexual stimulation is so thin that young football players have been known to achieve orgasm from the excitement of the game. The craziness of the sport sometimes affects players' ability to think rationally about their own safety. Last season Bears safety Shaun Gayle fractured the seventh vertebra in his neck when his helmet collided with teammate Singletary's hip during a tackle in a game against Detroit. Singletary had to come out of the game because of the collision, but Gayle stayed in, even though his neck was broken and his hands were numb. He dropped a ball he should have intercepted because he couldn't grip with his fingers, and still he remained in the game. He made another hit, on Lions fullback Garry James, and promptly lost feeling in his right arm. Still, he stayed in the game. Later, after he had been diagnosed and put on injured reserve for the rest of the season, he started working out at a health club I sometimes visit. I ran into him at the club and asked him how in the world he could have taken his own potential paralysis so lightly.

He laughed. Gayle is a bright man; he has a degree from Ohio State in recreation education and is one of the most well-spoken NFL players I have ever interviewed. But he just chuckled with the question.

"I didn't think it was that serious," he said.

Later I would read in the paper that Gayle was eagerly awaiting the 1989 season now that his neck had healed. "I will wear a built-in neck brace with my shoulder pads," he said. "It will allow me movement so I can see the ball but not much movement forwards or backwards. It should be interesting. I'll become a human missile."

I remember visiting Ohio State during the summer of 1987 to talk to all-American linebacker Chris Spielman about the coming season. Spielman, I knew, had been called "the most intense player I've ever coached" by then–head coach Earle Bruce. His father, Sonny Spielman, a high school football coach, recalled that when Chris was five years old he had tackled his own grandmother. "A perfect-form tackle," Dad said. " He broke her nose. He wiped her out on the spot. That's when I knew I had a maniac on my hands."

So I wanted to sit for a few minutes and just observe this athlete who against Iowa the previous year had broken his helmet, tossed it aside since there wasn't time to fix it, and dived into a pile headfirst. He sat in a coach's office at St. John's Hall and simply twitched. He was like a bug on a needle. I asked him what his style of play was and he said, "Controlled insanity." He added that what's important "is not how you play the game, it's whether you win or lose." He looked at the floor, avoided eye contact, bounced his knees. Playing Michigan, he said, was like freedom versus communism. "Football is almost a life or death situation for me," he said. Later, Chicago Bears quarterback Mike Tomczak, a teammate of Spielman's at Ohio State, would tell me that before each season Spielman would rent a room in a Cincinnati flophouse and simply lie on a bed for a day or two, staring at a bare light bulb hanging from the ceiling, getting his mind right for football.

I asked Spielman now if maybe things might not be a little easier for him if he weren't so totally focused on this violent game. He looked up.

"Easier for me, or the people around me?" he asked with an edge in his voice. "I have blinders on. I'm in a tunnel, a train is coming, and I don't see anything but the light approaching. That's how I want it."

A few years ago I was at the University of Pittsburgh to write about the Pitt team's response to the untimely death of sophomore linebacker Todd Becker. Becker was a special-teams demon, a 6′2″, 214-pound live wire with a tattoo on his left calf of a grinning Sylvester the Cat hanging Tweety Bird by the neck and whose favorite pastime, according to the Pitt press guide, was lifting weights. The young man had climbed out a third-story window at a dorm toga party to avoid detection by campus police who had raided the party, and when he tried to jump to the pavement thirty-five feet below, he spun in midair, hit his head on the cement, and died instantly. Becker was drunk at the time, but he also didn't think he could be hurt by the fall. "He had no fear," said head coach Foge Fazio. "I'm sure he thought, 'This is easy for me. I can do this.' " Becker's father,

Al, a long-distance trucker, said, ''He was such a good football player. He was a killer.''

But that same aggressiveness that delighted every coach Becker ever had got him into a lot of problems off the field. The reason Becker was jumping was that he had already been banned from the Pitt dorms for causing disturbances there and he didn't want to jeopardize his football career by getting caught again. In the course of researching my story, I spent some time with Pitt athletic director Ed Bozik, a former Air Force colonel, and during one interview he grew philosophical about the tragedy.

''Football training is very much analogous to military training,'' he said. ''In both cases young men are trained to do things they instinctively would not do. This has to condition your psyche, but the question is, can you convert that training and use its positive elements in normal life? In the military we have what we call 'war lovers,' the ones who can't turn it off. But everyone is constantly trained to act like gentlemen when not in a battle situation.

''Basically, I believe in the Aristotelian philosophy of striking a median, a balance. Any characteristic taken to an extreme becomes a vice. After all, getting into trouble, doing stupid things—that's not really the province of football players. It's traditional for *young people* to get into trouble.''

This is true, but when football players get into trouble, they just seem to do it a little harder, to take things a little further than other kids do, and this may be because the sport attracts, trains, conditions, and develops men who are predisposed to wildness and encourages them to push themselves beyond their limits. Perhaps Todd Becker would have done something equally stupid and self-destructive if he'd never heard of football. But were it not for football, he certainly wouldn't have been so praised and prized for these self-destructive tendencies, and he wouldn't have been so doggedly sought out by universities, by institutions of learning, eager to reward him for the qualities that led to his death: recklessness, fearlessness, aggressiveness.

Syndicated columnist Stephen Chapman has suggested getting rid of hard-shell helmets and imposing weight limits on players to lessen the violence of the game and the resulting injuries and unhealthy behavior such violence causes. But the helmets have been around for too long to downgrade, and ironically, they do prevent many of the head injuries that players in the olden days sometimes died from. And limiting the size of players would not be particularly effective in reducing violence, either, since speed is at least as devastating as weight in collisions. And in truth, many of the smaller players are the meanest players anyway. Safety Jack Tatum weighed just over 200 pounds when he paralyzed wide receiver Darryl Stingley with a vicious blow. And Detroit cornerback James Hunter weighed only 195 pounds when he nailed the Vikings' Ahmad Rashad and broke his back in 1982, ending Rashad's final season prematurely. Ironically, Hunter hit another Minnesota receiver in almost the same fashion later in the game and injured his own neck so severely from the blow that he himself was forced to retire.

I tried to contact Hunter after the '82 season to see what he thought about ending two careers in one game, but he wouldn't take my calls. I caught up with Rashad a year or so later in Miami, where he was preparing to work a Dolphins game as a TV reporter, and asked him what he felt about the incident.

"It was the weirdest pain I've ever had," he said. "I couldn't feel my legs for about five minutes. I was just like paralyzed. I told the trainer, 'When you get this helmet and these pads off me, I'll never play this game again.' "

What did he think of Hunter's blow to his back?

"I never thought it was too violent," Rashad answered. "I just got a good shot is all."

And there is the twisted truth that injuries are not only a

part of the game, but a welcome part. One of the very reasons players play the game is to have the chance to give *and receive* injuries. You think I'm kidding? I remember lying in bed after a college game with my own ankle throbbing, my shoulder aching, and feeling very . . . comfortable . . . about it all. The pain signified something. It wasn't the gratuitous pain of a disease or chronic illness, but a friendly, masculine reminder of my accomplishments as a player, and subliminally, as a man, in a dangerous sport.

"It's that instant when . . . artistry is threatened by violence and the outcome is in doubt, that epitomizes the game's attraction," wrote Oregon State English professor Mike Oriard in an essay on football violence in the *New York Times* a few years ago. "Injuries are not aberrations in football, or even a regrettable byproduct. They are essential to the game." He then added that any efforts to make the game safer must grapple first with the "ideological underpinning" of the game itself, since "it's not possible to have the (desired) danger without the injuries to confirm that the danger is real." Oriard had been a captain of the Notre Dame football team and had played four seasons with the Kansas City Chiefs in the early seventies. He was a center, and I remembered him from my brief stay with the Chiefs in 1971 as being a tall, quiet, observant man who did not seem to fit in with the rowdier, veteran Chiefs. If I had known the thinking going on in his brain, I might have made it a point to get to know him a little better before Hank Stram unceremoniously booted me out of pro football.

Pain itself is a funny bird. In an article on the matter in the June 11, 1984, edition of *Time,* pain researcher Dr. Ronald Dubner of the National Institutes of Health stated that "pain is a complex experience that involves emotions, previous experiences with pain, and what the pain means to us at any given time." "In short," concluded the article's author, "the borderline between the physiology and psychology of pain is a blurry one." Thus it is that, to a football player, pain can be something akin to rapture. I am reminded here of the saints of the Middle Ages, who likewise often got off on the self-inflicted pain that brought them closer to their God. One who stands out in particular was Henry Suso, a fourteenth-century saint who carved religious symbols in his chest with a stylus, wore a hair shirt, a heavy iron chain, and a tight-fitting hair undergarment with 150 nails imbedded in the straps, the points directed inward. Suso wore this gear at night, too, and when he picked at the outfit in his sleep, he had leather gloves made, fitted over with brass tacks, so that he could not enjoy the pleasure of touching himself. Suso mutilated himself to such an extent that according to historian Richard Kieckhefer, writing in *Unquiet Souls: Fourteenth-Century Saints and Their Religious Milieu,* ''suffering became for Suso almost an end in itself, or more precisely, a token of divine favor, such that an absence of suffering was for him the greatest cause of suffering.''

I can compare that nut to former Chiefs all-pro middle linebacker and center E. J. Holub, who, when I wrote about him for *Esquire* in 1980, was believed to have had more knee operations, twelve, than any other athlete in the world, with more cuttings scheduled for the future. Holub, a cowboy from West Texas, had undergone seventeen operations in all, including two on his hands, two on his elbows, and one on a hamstring, yet missed only eleven games in his eleven-year pro career. At forty-two, he walked like a man twice his age. Forget running. Holub destroyed his knees partly by coming back from the initial surgeries way too soon, once tearing off a cast almost three months before it was due to be removed. He would drain his knee joints himself, using a 16-gauge needle or sometimes a plain old razor. For a year with the Chiefs he wore a sanitary napkin on one knee to absorb the liquid that seeped out constantly.

''People are always asking me if it was worth it, the operations and all,'' he said to me cheerily. ''Yep, it sure was, I tell 'em. I enjoyed the hell out of football.''

There are many other players like Holub in the game, at all levels. Trust me. Tommy Chaikin told me one night about how he and some of his South Carolina teammates started drinking in his home while he was an undergrad and ended up carving each other's arms with a butcher knife in the kitchen, just for the hell of it, just to show pain was no big deal. They got a little carried away, stabbing one of the players pretty hard in the forearm. They went to bed after that, leaving the knife and blood on the table, forgetting that it might not be the pleasantest of sights for Tommy's parents in the morning. I found myself laughing, thinking back on some of my own lunacies in college. Looking back, I'm not particularly proud of that response.

Last fall I received a letter from a *Sports Illustrated* reader, and after reading it, I wrote back to its author, G. Bruce Mills of Lexington, North Carolina, asking him if I could print the letter in a book on college football that I was considering writing. Mills wrote back that he would be flattered to have his letter printed. Here it is:

> Dear Mr. Telander:
>
> After reading your story about Tommy Chaikin, I'm left asking a question to which I can't provide the answer: "What is it about football that drives participants to total disregard for their well-being in the quest for success?" Perhaps it's peer acceptance, or just a way to impress the girls. At my son's high school practice today I watched a player who was last in sprints (gasping for breath), struggled through drills, was hammered in the scrimmage, was the object of his teammates' ridicule, and will never get any better or make any contribution to his team. He's not alone, for practically every team at every level of amateur football has a player like him. Why do they do it? Why do the Tommy Chaikins of today risk their lives with drugs to achieve success in football?
>
> They're really no different from players of days gone by. I, like you, played college football in the late sixties and early seventies.

As an all-conference player at Duke University, I wasn't aware of this ''edge'' called steroids. But I, too, had an abusive addiction, which was playing with pain. At one time or another every player has been asked to ''suck it up,'' and doing anything less is unacceptable. Nobody wants to be told ''you can't cut it.'' I'll skip the details, but let it suffice to say that I've had four operations on my left knee, one on my right knee, two on my right ankle with the third scheduled for January. I must visit the chiropractor regularly for back pains, I walk clubfooted and struggle with inclines and rough terrain. I haven't been able to do anything resembling a jog or a run in four years, and my athletic sons are growing up without the benefit of playing backyard ball with their father.

The scariest thing, Rick, is that knowing what I've gone through and will continue to endure . . . I'D DO IT ALL OVER AGAIN! What is this mystical hold that football has over me and thousands like me?

I don't think anybody knows.

STRETCHING

There were four of them and they had become tight. Mostly, it was because they were the four starters in the secondary, but it was also because they thought alike. No, they didn't think alike. They probably wouldn't have been friends off the field. But they felt alike. They had the same feelings.

They practiced away from the rest of the team because they needed room for all their strange drills. Bull-in-the-ring, skeleton drills, tip drills, open-field tackling, unit coverage, rotation, support, recognition, and tons of man-to-man, just running all over the place like madmen trying to get to the ball before the receiver did. They had no idea what the offensive linemen did during most of practice. They didn't even play the same game as those guys. He had noticed that his team was not a team, really, but a conglomerate made up of parts that didn't have much to do with one another. It reminded him of a city, composed of neighborhoods. At times he felt like a citizen watching the city turn into a ghost town or flourish remarkably while he sat on the stoop. He saw the team as a snake, with undulations that might have little to do with the direction of the animal, but that propelled it relentlessly through the grass just the same.

The scrub wide receivers would run routes against them, and they'd try to read the scrubs' minds as they lined up. If they knew what the route was going to be, they would have to be tricky in the middle of the pattern, pretending not to know where it was going, so the receivers wouldn't adjust, but not faking it so well that they couldn't take advantage of their knowing. When the good receivers would get in the lines, the defensive backs would hesitate and fix their equipment so they could avoid matching up with certain players as much as possible. Another thing he had discovered: If a receiver is good enough, you can't cover him. You need help.

In one game the other cornerback came back to the huddle, a strange look in his eyes. "Did you see number one fly!" he said to him. "Jesus H. Christ."

The wide receiver came to his side, and he was a blur. He hadn't been on the scouting report, so they didn't know he existed. So he started lining up ten yards deep whenever number one came to his side. He let him sprint straight. Luckily, the man showed no ability to cut in any direction, and they were able to handle him pretty well just with their cushions. Later, they found out he was a track man who held the world record in one of the indoor dashes. They held nothing.

In another game, the four of them were defending against a complicated flood pattern, each trying to do his job but aware of the others. The ball went up and they all converged and came crashing down within a few yards of each other. Their coverage was perfect. He had a warm feeling. There were times like this when things worked out right, and it was plain that the whole was much greater than the parts.

CHAPTER 6

College Football Promotes the Values America Needs

I was sitting here at my desk, reading the *Chicago Tribune* absentmindedly, thinking about ethics, duty, morality, and some of the vague, camels-through-the-eyes-of-needles metaphysics that we always hope can shed some dim light on what we ought to do in life. I don't mean whether or not a man should become a singer or a carpenter or whether he should buy government bonds or rare paintings—not that kind of "ought to do." Rather, I mean what a person ought to do in the grand scheme of things, what kind of a statement a person should make regarding life and his passage through it, particularly with regard to his relationship with his fellow travelers, his children, his loved ones, his enemies, mankind. It's the kind of reverie that can put one to sleep or dredge up frightening flashbacks of two A.M. dormitory debates over the validity of Dostoevsky's Grand Inquisitor and other banalities. I was drifting hither and yon, pondering how the corruption of college football could ever have led me into such filmy abstractions, when I found myself reading an article in the paper about the loss of values in the United States and the resulting demise in the structure of the family as well as the declining happiness and mental health of our children, and things started to fall into place.

"We've helped weaken the family and left it unable to deal with crises," said Dr. Thomas Todd, the chief psychologist at Forest PsychCare Hospital in Des Plaines, Illinois, one of the top child psychiatric facilities in the state. By "we," Dr. Todd meant the social sciences field specifically and the American people generally. "We took away all these vitally important things from our culture: religion, common sense, tradition. And we didn't replace those things with anything of real value. We promoted the value-neutral society. That is the crisis. Kids are on drugs. Families are collapsing. The roots are gone. That is why we see so many children in our wards."

The issue of a valueless society was expanded upon in the article by Dr. James Egan, the chief of child and adolescent psychiatry at Children's Hospital in Washington, D.C. Egan noted that the anything-goes attitudes of the 1970s have come back to haunt us in the moral bankruptcy that heralds our entrance into the 1990s. "What we did is that we removed the idea of judgment from any discussion in our homes, schools, politics, and government," said Egan. "We replaced it with charts and graphs and a superior sense of objectivity. For decades, we've told everyone not to judge, not to establish rights and wrongs. And over the long haul, what that's done is work to weaken and destroy the foundations of our families and ultimately the culture we knew." Dr. Derek Miller, the director of child and adolescent psychiatry at Northwestern Memorial Hospital in Chicago and one of the nation's experts on troubled children, added that that elimination of judgment as a moral pathway now torments parents and children alike. "Depression-era parents didn't want their children to have to sacrifice anything; they gave them whatever the children wanted," he said. "The parents of today were given free rein, with little or no limits set for them. They indulged themselves, and they continue to do so. So today's parents don't set limits for their own children. Our biggest problem is teaching parents how to be parents. How can a culture retrain itself?''

How can a culture retrain itself. What a question! Think of that; it's like asking how a pair of cowboy boots can turn themselves back into a living, breathing alligator. A culture is what we are, what we have become through our own choices.

And yet, within that question lies the problem that is destroying the little world of college football as well. The sport is, like parenting, an institution that has lost its way. It needs to retrain itself. Parents have indulged themselves; the rulers and fans of college football have indulged themselves. When parenting stumbles and starts to embody greed and the fulfillment of private desires and not the betterment of the family and society, there is a harrowing ripple effect that washes over the innocent, the children. The same is true of big-time college football. When it puts its own concerns as a greedy, self-indulgent, exploitive, and valueless institution above the interests of its players, and by ripple effect, other young people and the ethics of our society as a whole, then you have the corruption of the innocent. And you've got a problem.

Oh, I know I'm wrapped up in this thing and blinded by my closeness to it and that there's a revolution going on in China and clear-cutting of the rain forests in Brazil and hyperinflation in Argentina and starvation in the Sudan and very strange times indeed in the USSR, and that on the canvas of the big ethical picture the scale of college football's shadow is very small. But what goes on in college football is important, very important. Even if you're like so many professors at so many universities who simply turn their noses from the stench and say, ''Sports are dumb, I will ignore them,'' you are affected by the corruption all the same. Big-time college football proves to all students—and ultimately, all of us—that no matter what anybody says, winning, money, and entertainment are our gods. Knowledge, truth, integrity? They're okay—in their place. But let's not let them get in the way of what's really important.

Before we ask what we ought to do, we have to understand why we're doing what we're doing right now. How did this thing called big-time college football get here in the first place? And who are we perpetuating it for?

I hope in the previous chapters I've explained a little bit about how college football arrived at its current station, that its journey has been that of a runaway train that was always headed in the wrong direction and has gained speed in recent times and is fast approaching the end of the tracks. Later, I'll have a little bit more to say about football's history, but right now let's see if we can figure out why the train continues with such speed.

As we've seen, the games are certainly no longer played for the sake of the players or, in most cases, for the faculty. From what I have seen, I can tell you the games are not played for the students, either; I saw so many Ohio State students hawking their tickets to a recent Buckeyes home game that I wondered if the student passes were issued by the school simply as a way to bolster students' income. At a recent Nebraska-Oklahoma game in Lincoln, I got almost no sense that this was a college event, only that thousands of adults can descend on a campus and overrun it like bright red locusts. In truth, students actually attending college football games and caring deeply about what happens on the field are now nearly as rare as raccoon coats.

And more and more, the universities are blatantly saying the hell with the students anyway by scheduling games before classes start, during vacations, and in distant states and foreign countries. Just yesterday I got an invitation in the mail to attend the second annual Emerald Isle Classic between Pittsburgh and Rutgers to be held December 2, 1989, at Landsdown Road Stadium in Dublin, Ireland. Wonder how many students will be at that one? There are plans for Southern Cal and Illinois to play in a Glasnost Bowl in Moscow, and Western Carolina is looking for an opponent to play in an as-yet-untitled wingding in Toulouse, France.

Georgia Tech won't be playing in France, but only because the promoters wouldn't pay them a $175,000 guarantee for their trouble. Of course, good old Tech is about as up-front money-hungry as even your greediest corporation, and it's found a whole new way to rake in the cash: The Ramblin' Wrecks are selling corporate sponsors chips for all of their home games, with a price of $75,000 being suggested for contests against Maryland, North Carolina, Virginia, Wake Forest, and Western Carolina; $100,000 for Boston College; and $175,000 for the season finale against archrival Georgia. "When you look at the money in corporate sponsorship, it's absolutely unbelievable," says Kevin Bryant, the director of marketing and promotions for the school. No, Kevin, it's the extent to which a fine academic institution will prostitute itself that's absolutely unbelievable.

So if the games aren't for the players, the faculty, or the students, what we are left with is the notion that the big-time college game is played primarily for nonstudent fans and alumni. Let's toss out the nonstudent fans as a factor, since what they want should be of little concern to an institution that calls education its primary function. And while we're at it, let's forget for the moment about the wishes of coaches, athletic-department personnel, TV executives, and NCAA and CFA brass, since what they want in this matter is transparent as glass. How about these alums, these masses of former students with checkbooks and clout; is the game played for them?

There isn't much evidence to support a claim one way or the other on this issue, but in an article published in the December 1981 edition of *CASE Currents,* a journal for college fundraising, development, and media relations officers, our old buddy Dr. James H. Frey notes that in the one in-depth scientifically controlled study done on alumni opinion about university athletics, there is no indication that the vast majority of alums care about big-time sport at all. In fact, the study—a 1972 poll of 800 randomly selected Washington State University alumni, with a 90 percent response—shows that most alums care far more about academic programs and extracurricular activities such as recreation, dramatics, and music than they do about the football team. The only disagreement in the study came between the few alumni leaders and the general alumni body in their respective attitudes regarding big-time sport.

"Alumni leaders rated athletics much more highly than did rank-and-file alumni," wrote Frey. "Actually, few alumni have any significant input into athletic policy. Most of them, in fact, think athletics are not all that important, particularly when compared to the need for other programs of higher education.

"The low priority assigned athletics by the general alumni body contradicts the myth that 'alumni demand winning and/or competitive athletic teams.' This statement reflects the opinions of a few select alumni leaders rather than the general alumni body.

"The survey also indicates that many if not most alumni would like to participate in events of a nonathletic, academic, or vocational nature. From this you can infer that many alumni may not be making gifts to the university simply because it overemphasizes athletics."

I have not spent much time searching for alumni-opinion studies that may have been conducted since Frey's article appeared, and I suppose it is possible that college alums all of a sudden have turned into rabid football fans, but I doubt it. That study has the ring of truth to it, then and now. It documents what I think I have seen with my own two eyes—that there is a small but powerful and vocal group of alumni at all big-time football institutions who promote the football program, drown out opposition, and get what they want. From what I've seen, I would say that those groups are composed largely of big-shot businessmen, a number of whom previously played football for the school in question, and who consider the football team to be an extension of their aggressive and largely successful forays into the world of money-making and power-wielding.

If the study and Frey and I are correct, then universities are being led into ethical hell by a few loudmouth, big-walleted jerks. And the pathetic part is that the universities simply allow it to happen. I can understand that alumni who are not supporters of big-time football would generally be quiet about the matter—who, after all, makes a big stink about something they disapprove of but that is both distant and apparently unobtrusive in their day-to-day lives? But how do the university administrators explain their failure to rally support and regain control of their programs?

"It is often less than honest to justify university policy and action by citing 'alumni opinion,' " writes Frey. "Assertions such as 'we must maintain or increase alumni support' or 'alumni pressure forces us to emphasize football' are simply designed to defuse pressure from groups adversely affected by certain decisions. In other words, administrators often use alumni opinion as a convenient scapegoat. In any event, universities . . . know little about their alumni. They presume opinions, beliefs, and preferences, yet they almost never conduct scientific research into the matter."

In other words, college presidents are willing to be led by noisemakers, to take the road of least resistance. In other words, they are shirking their duties as educators.

It is amusing to see what happens when a president does get fed up and takes a stand that is counter to the best interests of the football program. The University of Iowa's Hunter Rawlings did just that last winter when he recommended that the NCAA ban freshman athletes from its football teams, adding that if the organization did not do that in three years, Iowa itself would unilaterally make the move. Rawlings made the statement after his embarrassment at learning through the Norby Walters–Lloyd Bloom trial that some of his football players were not what you would call real students, that, for instance, in his last semester at Iowa in 1986 defensive back Devon Mitchell enrolled in five classes, withdrew from four, and got an incomplete in First Aid and CPR. Still, many Iowans were outraged at the proposal, calling for Rawlings's resignation. Coach Hayden Fry threatened to quit. The *Des Moines Register* conducted a poll that showed that 74 percent of its readers objected to Rawlings's proposal. It also showed that only 13 percent of those people who claimed to be University of Iowa football fans had ever taken a class at the school.

I don't know how far Rawlings has had to backtrack on his proposal, but I do know that if he kowtows to nonstudents and nonalumni while making school policy, he should ask himself why he's president of a university in the first place. Maybe he's utterly baffled and unnerved by Iowa governor Terry Branstad, who argued against Rawlings's proposal and then flat-out admitted that college football is not just a university function. Football, said the governor, "is very important and significant" at "larger universities." Beyond that, he said, it is "a source of entertainment for many people who never went to college themselves."

And there you have it. Big-time college football is entertainment for anybody who needs something to keep him amused in the fall. That is its purpose in our society. University of Minnesota president Kenneth Keller beat Branstad to the punch when he told the special convention of the NCAA in 1987, "We in Division I are in an entertainment business and we can't fool ourselves." At the time, I admired Keller for being so honest, but I also wondered how in the world he could state that truism without being in a fit of rage, or at least being too embarrassed to continue his speech. It is this role as entertainer to the public that has made universities as unethical as plagiarists—and it is the presidents who have allowed it to happen.

I continue on with my newspaper reading, turn to *The Sporting News,* and find that three of the last four rushing champions in the Atlantic Coast Conference have been arrested for crimes ranging from alleged theft to cocaine possession and conspiracy to distribute cocaine. One of the rushers was initially charged with murder in one of the cases, but the charge was dropped for insufficient evidence. I see that Washington State has held nineteen players out of spring practice for academic reasons, an action prompted by the team's cumulative D-plus average last fall. Interestingly, one of the players who was forced to miss the drills was second-team all-American running back Rich Swinton. Swinton was a National Merit Scholar in high school and considered attending Harvard before coming to WSU. I find myself wondering if Swinton and the others were in any way affected by the hypocrisy and immorality of the system engulfing them, if it might in any way have made their transgressions easier to commit. No, I don't wonder—I know it did. It makes it easier for all of us.

One of the common responses to the current ills in big-time college football is to say that what we need to do is get back to the way things used to be, that in that indistinct realm known as "back then" college football was clean and pure. It is a seductive trap, but the notion is both wrong and dangerous. It is wrong because big-time college football has always been corrupt, though it was certainly less glaringly offensive than in today's era of TV, steroids, and weight machines. And it is dangerous because it implies that the solution to college football's woes lies in a reactionary response, that by somehow returning to the presumed integrity of an innocent past we can make everything right once again. But if history has proven anything, it is that we can't go back, even if things in the old days really were better. We can never again pretend that we don't know how to make nuclear bombs, for instance. But in college football's case, if we were to return to the past, we would have to change some epic events outside the sport itself to maneuver the game into the place it now should be. Prime among those events is the Civil War.

While working on this book I had the good fortune to discover a young man named James Weeks, a doctoral candidate in history at Penn State University. Weeks wrote his dissertation on the Civil War and its influence on the new American sport known as football. I had read an excerpt from his work in *American Heritage Magazine* and felt compelled to track him down to pick his brain a little further. I found him at the university, and after a couple of long and provocative phone conversations, he sent me his original paper, entitled: "From Appomattox to the Gridiron; The Civil War's Influence on the Rise of Football."

In the paper he points out that the War Between the States, though a hideously gruesome and demoralizing affair that killed more people than any other war in our history, in time became the romantic linchpin that made football an integral part of the college world. In much the same way that the American public has dealt with the unsettling realities of the Vietnam War—first denying the event, then reluctantly accepting it, then romanticizing it—so, too, did late-nineteenth-century Americans handle the Civil War. At first no one wanted to talk about the conflict, but gradually, writes Weeks, "a transformation in sentiment toward the war occurred beginning in the 1880s. For veterans, the painful recollection of misery faded, framing instead an image of self-sacrifice, heroism, and duty. A return to dull routine in an increasingly systemized society highlighted the war's adventure for veterans as the best years of their lives."

Then something even more remarkable happened: The leaders and shapers of the nation began also to see the Civil War through rose-colored glasses, and they designated this new game of football as the war's everyday equivalent. "In football," writes Weeks, "the nation discovered a convenient instrument of 'the strenuous life,' a doctrine linked by many of the war generation to a revivification of Civil War spirit." Men of letters began to praise the ennobling aspects of football at the same time and in the same spirit that they praised the war. In his 1895 address to Harvard's graduating class, future Supreme Court justice Oliver Wendell Holmes, who believed heartily in the need for men to be "manly," declared, "Out of heroism grows faith in the worth of heroism. . . . Therefore I rejoice at every dangerous sport which I see pursued.'' The ''Sis-Boom-Bah'' cheer that we still sometimes hear at college football games springs from the post–Civil War sporting crowd's verbalization of a rocket soaring and exploding on enemy troops and the firing army's subsequent roar of approval.

At the turn of the century Teddy Roosevelt made the deification of the sport complete. Though he would later come to consider banning football entirely because of its danger both ethically and physically, in the beginning he sang its praises as a man-builder for collegians. ''Roosevelt idolized those who fought in the Civil War,'' Weeks explained over the phone. ''He wanted to repeat the gallantries he associated with that war in the Spanish-American War, which he was in. He rode up San Juan Hill, but it was just jingoism. But he wrote that football could build the same character that one supposedly built in war.''

Sport suffers whenever people ascribe their own moral dogma to its process. Clearly, football should not be war any more than it should be religion. Nothing is war but war itself. ''I'll tell you what war is all about,'' General Curtis LeMay said in 1953. ''You've got to kill people, and when you've killed enough, they stop fighting.'' Football is brutal, but it is a game, which is why there are rules and a clock governing it.

Perhaps we have needed all this time to realize what football is and is not, and whether it can help us as human beings. Many people will tell you that football teaches players how to compete ferociously and then get ahead in this dog-eat-dog world. They will invariably add that competition is what the world is all about, that you gotta be tough, and that only the strong survive. But the whole notion of competition as an adversarial battle may not be correct. In a recent essay on competition, noted sports author George Leonard writes, ''The worthy opponent is integral to the play, not an enemy but a coconspirator. The conspiracy is revealed in the word *compete* itself, which comes from two Latin roots, *com* and *petere,* 'to seek together.' In this light, competition may be seen as a secret form of cooperation." Leonard goes on to note a seeming paradox at the root of competition, the fact that to get the most out of any game, one must play all out to win, while at the same time not letting an obsession with winning ruin one's pleasure in the game itself. "The ultimate athlete," he writes, "is one who resolves this seeming contradiction by playing graciously, and more often than not by winning." Seen in this light, competition has one mortal enemy: cheating. Thus, the incessant—nay, necessary—cheating that goes along with big-time college football deals a crushing blow to the natural pleasure of competition as well as the formation of character.

In an essay in *Sports Illustrated* on the same topic, competition, writer Bil Gilbert explains in greater depth that competition is a vital element to sport, but not life in general. Cooperation, rather than "the win-or-drop-dead, tennis-tournament model of evolution" is how we have gotten to this point in our history, he states. A good argument can be made, he continues, "that life is mostly about *avoiding* competition. If this is so, then competitive sports jump out not only as a remarkable exception but also as a singular, perhaps definitive, human activity." Thus, sports are not like life at all. Because they have been fancifully created, they transcend and even disregard the rules of the world, which is why they are pleasurable. Things get fouled up, in football and all sports, when hypocrisy steps into this pristine arrangement. In his essay, Gilbert talks to legendary former UCLA basketball coach John Wooden to see if this sage can help him better understand the function of competition. "The question comes up frequently, so I asked various authorities whether they thought competitive sports were good or bad for people," writes Gilbert. "Wooden answered succinctly. 'You are probably asking about character,' he said. 'Yes, I think competition can build character. But it can also tear it down.' "

Certainly, this is true, and much depends on the people playing the games and the pressures placed upon them as they compete. Still, we will always feel that elite sport is worth the risk of injury or failure because of the potential good and pleasure the sport can bring. That is why we want regulatory bodies to keep sports functioning smoothly and to step in and restore order in times of crisis. Such is the role we want the National Collegiate Athletic Association to play in the world of big-time college football. Let me tell you why it doesn't.

No, first, let me tell you how I feel on a very primitive, visceral level about the NCAA: *I hate it.* There is, I must confess, something about an organization that employs a lot of people whose duty is to govern others with whom they have almost nothing in common that irritates me no end. I see the NCAA's leaders as a bunch of know-nothing, self-righteous stuffed suits who are willing to do just enough labor to keep the organization running forever. That's my prejudice, and having stated it, let me now set it aside and explain without bias why the NCAA can never bring integrity to the sport.

To begin with, the NCAA was not created to do any such thing. It exists for four basic purposes: First, it was set up to establish rules for the game of football itself, so that all colleges under its wing would play the same game. Secondly, it was set up to act as a cartel for bargaining purposes. (The success of that unified approach was apparent on the last day that Congress was in session last year when it approved a revision of the 1986 tax law to permit an 80-percent tax deduction for contributions to college athletic programs, even when the contributions entitle the donor to preference in purchasing choice seats at sporting events. Pay big bucks, get nice seats, write it off. It was a political and economic coup worthy of the toughest of Washington lobbyists.) Third, the NCAA was designed to deal with whatever outside forces might enter its sphere. In that regard, the NCAA has for years worked a silent arrangement with the NFL wherein the pro league scouts college players and picks them in an orderly draft with the NCAA's blessing, in return for which the NFL agrees not to take NCAA players before their eligibility has expired. Fourth, the NCAA serves as a central public relations outlet, devoted to noble-sounding declarations about the righteous qualities of its member institution. It is no accident that the NCAA spends far more on PR and promotions than it does on enforcement of the rules that exist to safeguard the sport's alleged integrity.

Listen to the sanctimonious quotes that the NCAA spews forth and try not to think of ostriches. "Our real purpose is to prepare student athletes to be major contributors to our society," says Dick Schultz, "while also providing meaningful opportunities for intercollegiate athletics." Excuse me if I cough. "Ninety-nine percent of everything that's going on in intercollegiate athletics is exceptionally positive," says Schultz. "We have to be sure we don't get mired down in that one percent that's negative."

Dear me. Let's make sure we don't get distracted when the University of Washington's Don James recruits a star San Diego high school running back named Marc Jones and then signs him following Jones's release after spending seven months in prison for the brutal beating and partial blinding of another man. James justified it all by saying, "His background is probably better than most players we bring in." Or when Senator Bill Bradley, a former NCAA basketball star, tries to get the NCAA to approve an innocuous bill that would require schools to release graduation rates for scholarship athletes—so recruits can make informed decisions about the places where they will be getting their educations—and the NCAA shrieks as though Bradley has asked members to line up for body tattoos. Bradley stated that he was "absolutely flabbergasted by the opposition" of the organization, but those of us who know the NCAA a little better would never have expected the NCAA to give up anything resembling power or clout without a battle.

The real function of the NCAA is to promote a good image of itself, make money, and protect the status quo. No doubt NCAA brass would squawk that such is not the case, that they remain ever vigilant for fraud and corruption in the college game, but protecting their own hides is what it's really all about. And it's foolish to expect them to do much else.

I was thinking about this exact subject yesterday when I ventured out of my office to get some fresh air and a cup of coffee in the little square that passes for the business center in this town. I ran into Mike McCaskey, the president of the Chicago Bears, and we sat on a bench in the square and talked for a while about football and ethics. He asked me what I thought about the way the Bears had released popular veteran linebacker Otis Wilson. Wilson had a damaged knee and other physical problems including a bad back, and the Bears had dumped him after last season without even giving him a chance to show whether he could still play for the team. "We were trying to help him," McCaskey said.

I shrugged and said I didn't believe him, that even if it was for Otis Wilson's own good, it was more for the Bears' own good, but that it wasn't really important, anyway, since the NFL is not about being nice. Pro football is a mean, cutthroat, heartbreaking business, at least for the players, and they all know that going in. Owners, hey, they're the kids who own the bats and balls and postgame snacks; they can do whatever they want.

I told him that I was writing a book about the corruption of college football, and that I specifically had not gone after the pro game because no matter how unfair it might be, it pretty much keeps its unfairness out in the open where we all can see it. McCaskey chuckled, not from relief, but because whenever we talk, I always end up pontificating while he sits silently like a fox. I remembered then that in this very chapter I planned to use something from the book he had given me a few years ago, the one he had written while he was a business professor at Harvard. Its title is *The Executive Challenge: Managing Change and Ambiguity,* and it deals with the ways a business manager can try to stay afloat in troubled times. The thing sounds about as interesting as a treatise on the eating habits of slugs, I know, but for some reason I found the book intriguing and enjoyable and pertinent to the real world, and I read it all at once as though it were a spy thriller.

I told him that his section on the Navy's reaction to the invention of the continuous-aiming gun at the turn of the century had a direct parallel in the NCAA's current response to the manifest corruption of college football. I said that it was a lesson about human nature that applied, most probably, across time and culture. He smiled as to if to say, how quaint, which sort of ticked me off, since he had written the story in the first place and knew good and well what it had to do with the actions of people in power generally, and of an organization like the NCAA in particular. But maybe inscrutability works well when dealing with highly paid athletes, and maybe McCaskey knows things about influencing underlings that he doesn't divulge in the book. At any rate, I can give you McCaskey's parable of self-protection as he constructed it from Elting Morison's history of the adoption of continuous-aim firing in the United States Navy, and I think you'll see the pertinence of its message to the behavior of the NCAA in its attitude toward football:

> First devised by an English officer in 1898, this system allowed a ship's gun to be continuously aimed and readjusted as it was being fired. A U.S. Navy lieutenant stationed in China, William Sims, learned about the system from its originator, Percy Scott of the British Royal Navy. With Scott's assistance, Sims had the system installed on an American ship and trained a crew to use it. After a few months, the American crew showed the same remarkable improvement in accuracy as the British crews had. Sims wrote thirteen official reports, complete with great masses of data, to naval officers in Washington arguing the merits of the new system.
>
> At first Washington officials made no response. According to their conceptual maps [''map'' is McCaskey's term for one's

> personal vision of reality] of naval gunnery, Sims's claims simply were not credible. As Sims became deliberately challenging and shocking in his reports, officials began to rebut the claims. They argued that existing American equipment was as good as British equipment and that any deficiencies must lie in the training of the men. They also conducted gunnery practice *on dry land* where, deprived of the benefits of the inertial movement, their results *proved* that the new system could not work as Sims claimed. They called Sims a "crackbrain egoist" and accused him of deliberately falsifying evidence.
>
> Not to be denied, Sims, who had the combative personality of a bantam rooster, circulated news of the new gunnery system among his fellow officers in the fleet. Finally in 1902, he took the bold step of writing directly to President Theodore Roosevelt. Roosevelt brought Sims back from China and forced change upon the Navy by installing Sims as Inspector of Target Practice.
>
> [The] Navy had its own reasons for resisting the technological innovation. The officers in Washington identified strongly with the existing equipment and their instinctive desire was to protect the established pecking order of the Navy. Intuitively they realized that the Navy's social system was organized around its major weapons systems and that a change would significantly disrupt the existing hierarchy of status. Indeed, the chaos of subsequent events proved this fear justified. [The] Washington officers sought to protect their map and the culture in which it was embedded. They held on to the map as long as possible and only let go when forced to do so by greater, outside authority.

What the event demonstrated so neatly is that what people say their goals are, and what those goals really are, are quite often two very different things. If you had asked any Navy officer in Sims's day what his goal was regarding his work, that officer most certainly would have replied that it was to serve the United States well and protect our citizenry from harm by the best means available to the Navy, which would have included using the most advanced and effective weaponry available. While the officer may actually have felt he believed that statement, his actions would have betrayed him. Certainly, he wanted to do those things he mentioned, but only if they did not disrupt his own comfortable, safe, and understandable private world. Generally, people don't want change for any reason, and when a person is confronted with the possibility of change—even when the change will benefit a great many people—the person will, as McCaskey says, "fight to protect what is familiar and known—and to maintain identity, status, income, and standing."

The NCAA doesn't want to change. It doesn't want to legislate itself virtually out of existence. It has 292 Division I and 503 Division II and III schools as members, and just like the old Navy, everything is nice and tidy just the way it is, thank you. An ethical housecleaning would turn the whole chummy system into chaos, even if it ultimately brought integrity to the game. So let's forget about the NCAA as being anything other than an anchor against progress.

These times we live in are different. The world is now a truly global community where actions in one part rapidly affect matters on the other side of the world. Money and its resulting power flow back and forth across once sovereign national borders without heed to the governments below. It may be true, as some economists have suggested, that countries themselves are losing their power and that multinational corporations are the new leadership forces to be reckoned with. In light of these changes it naturally occurs that some things that once seemed to have a place in our lives no longer do. I am thinking of the idealistic notion that what Holmes praised as "dangerous sport"—like football—has a valid role to play in the higher education of young men. In *The Liberal Education,* published in 1937, author and former Lawrence University president Henry Merritt Wriston wrote exuberantly of that role, claiming that those "vigorous and competitive sports belong peculiarly in the liberal college, for its ideal is an adventurous philosophy of life. Mere physical survival is not enough; the goal is life enriched by experience, even the experience of pain. . . . I know of no youthful experience equal to football and other sports in bringing the fact of pain into its right perspective.''

But even Wriston was disgusted by the growing commercialization and hypocrisy of the sport. ''Honest professionalism is beyond criticism,'' he wrote. ''But to pretend that . . . one is cultivating the liberal ideal of life is just sheer hypocrisy, and nothing destroys integrity of character so rapidly or so completely. The institution which exploits youth for profit or for publicity betrays its calling; it impairs or destroys its capacity to fulfill its true function.''

Amen.

Interestingly, as I was delving through the mounds of papers I have collected for this book, I came upon a *Washington Post* story about the NCAA special convention held in Dallas in 1987. That session was heralded as ''the first national debate on the proper role of intercollegiate athletics in higher education,'' and everybody from college presidents to college chancellors to college football coaches got a chance to speak his piece. After one university president meekly suggested that colleges might do well to create fewer incentives to win and lessen the drive to make profits off their big-time teams, a vehement rebuttal was tossed out by then-president of the University of Oklahoma, Frank Horton.

Aha, I thought, here is the guy I've been meaning to get hold of. Horton is the man who quietly left OU last fall to go to the University of Toledo, and I'd heard that he had tried to harness the Sooners' full-tilt sports program and had been sacked for his efforts. His departure seemed to carry all the earmarks of martyrdom—at least as I interpreted it from the stories told me by University of Miami (Ohio) president Paul Pearson and others.

Horton told the 1987 assembly that big schools should have freedom of choice to pursue big-time sport. ''It is hypocritical to believe a college with a visible athletic program is less interested in its academic reputation,'' he said. ''No school is better or worse because of the level of competition it desires. Don't legislate mediocrity. Let us not legislate Division I-A into Division III and Division III into Division XI.''

I called Horton at Toledo and asked him why, exactly, he had left Oklahoma. ''I did some things that are in my best interest,'' he said. ''I really don't want to say any more. I've made my statement.''

I asked him if he wasn't disgusted by all the problems that have occurred with the Oklahoma football program in recent times.

To my surprise, he said that he didn't think that what was happening with any big-time football programs anywhere in the country was that unusual or reprehensible. ''Was it sports that created these problems?'' he asked. ''There are issues in society that sports are not exempt from. But when it's associated with athletics, then it becomes a major issue. But it is just *part* of society.''

What about the Zarek Peters shooting? What about the quarterback selling cocaine? What about handguns and ammunition in a university athletic dorm? Are those things normal?

''I don't know that there aren't rounds of ammunition in any dorm in America, generally,'' he replied.

To say he wasn't giving the responses I had expected would be an understatement.

''Don't get me wrong,'' he added. ''I don't condone that kind of behavior. But if the person who shot the other was a doctor, would you condemn all doctors?''

Horton's words stayed with me. They kept reminding me how hard we fight the realization that the problem here is profound and fundamental and won't respond to quick fixes and shortcut cures. The problem is so big, but the solutions people propose are so small, that it's clear they just don't understand. Recently, Texas governor Bill Clements, who two years ago publicly apologized for his role in the payoff scandal that earned Southern Methodist's football program the death penalty, signed a bill that makes it a crime to recruit college athletes with money or gifts in Texas. The new law makes payoffs to athletes a third-degree felony, punishable by two to ten years in prison and a fine up to $5,000. A student-athlete who solicits or takes money would be charged with a misdemeanor under the same ruling and liable to as much as a year in jail and a $2,000 fine. Though possibly well-intentioned, the law is a bizarre mishmash growing out of the money-grubbing chaos that has made a shambles of the Southwest Conference and the deep-rooted protectionism of Texas football fans. The law can send athletes and boosters to jail for taking or offering cash to play football, but only if such acts occur on Texas soil. Thus, an Oklahoma backer from Norman who drives to, say, Lubbock to woo a Texas high-school star with cash can get nailed for a felony, but a University of Texas booster who goes to Oklahoma City to steal a player from the Sooners with a similar offer is safe and clean. As Representative Pete Laney, who sponsored the bill in the Texas House, stated, "Oklahoma could come into Texas and risk not getting caught while they were in Texas. But this [making the booster's crime a felony rather than a misdemeanor] will fix Oklahoma, too, because you can be extradited from Oklahoma for violating this law in Texas."

The law wasn't even supported by the NCAA, which said that it would only make its own enforcement efforts more difficult because the severity of the Texas punishment would most likely make sources reluctant to talk to investigators. Ironically, if the bill had been law back in 1984, it probably could have been used to send Governor Clements himself to prison for his role in the SMU mess. "I think it would have made a criminal liability for him," said Senator Bob Glasgow, who sponsored the bill in the Senate.

A different approach is being taken in Nebraska, where a bill proposed to the state legislature would make the NCAA liable for damages when penalties against football or basketball programs at one school result in revenue losses or disrupt athletic programs *at other schools*. The University of Nebraska figured it could lose as much as half a million dollars a year due to canceled TV and bowl games stemming from NCAA sanctions against Oklahoma and Oklahoma State. "I think some recent cases have made people wake up and realize that when the NCAA punishes one school, it can result in many other schools being punished as well," said Nebraska senator Ernie Chambers.

Neither Horton nor Clements nor Chambers is even considering the possibility that the whole concept of money-making big-time collegiate football is wrong and unethical. Laws such as the ones above will only make the mess more tangled and incomprehensible. How blind and selfish can you be to sue the NCAA for damages for putting member schools that have broken its laws on probation? What is the NCAA supposed to do—reward wrongdoers? When people refuse to acknowledge the corruption of the whole sport, they force themselves into tortured logic and finally, more and more hypocrisy as they attempt to stop bullets with flyswatters.

At the same 1987 NCAA special convention, Lawrence University president Rik Warch, a man who admits he has an advantage in perspective by running a Division III school, said, "I believe we should not focus on the few bad actors and alleged renegade institutions and seek ways to control or punish their behavior. That approach will lead us only to consider various policing and sanctioning provisions and will distract us from attending to the fundamental issues." Rather, Warch concluded, universities must go for radical reform in the structure of intercollegiate sport so as to "reinforce the primary qualities of our colleges and universities in their service to students."

He is right, and what he is asking is for people with vested interests in big-time football—governors, boards of regents, presidents, athletic directors, coaches, media moguls, fans, boosters, alumni—to put aside those interests and do what is right for once. Not to do so is, in its way, a form of aggression that has the youth of this country as its primary victims.

In the course of writing this book I have been thinking a lot about aggression, and at times I have drifted back to my college days and begun pondering some of the old lessons I picked up in those seemingly impractical and unusable humanities courses. I remember the book *On Aggression,* by Konrad Lorenz, and I see now that it had much truth in it. The world has changed, Lorenz said, and the aggression that once served our species well in its battle against saber-toothed tigers and woolly mammoths is now no longer needed for our survival. We have to control that aggression and carefully direct it and defuse it for our species to benefit. And this, he added, could be accomplished by the use of reason, humor, and the contemplation of other species as we slog through our daily lives.

Again digging through my voluminous paper heap, I happened upon a yellowing newspaper article recording an interview with Lorenz in Vienna in early 1984. An old yet vigorous man then, Lorenz was asked by the interviewer if he still believed all the things he had written in *On Aggression,* published twenty-three years earlier.

"I don't retract anything," Lorenz said. "I haven't changed my opinion in any part of what I wrote in that book." Then he added, "Man is worse than I thought him to be when I wrote that book. If anything, I underrated the dangers from human aggressiveness."

Lorenz did not sound terminally depressed by this knowledge but rather tentatively hopeful that, given the message, man could yet tame himself. Lorenz was raising wild pigs, geese, and coral fish at his institute in Vienna; and perhaps symbolically, he also bred endangered species of owls and hawks. "I'm now eighty years old," he said ("grandly, leaning on his walking stick," according to the report). "And I have more or less the duty to say what I believe and what I think I know without any hesitation.''

I am half his age and have one-tenth his brainpower, but when it comes to the subject of big-time college football, I think I also need to say what I think I know, without any more hesitation.

STRETCHING

They were not a very talented group, but they played well together.

There had been only a couple of serious injuries all season, the seniors had worn the mantle of leadership well, and the team had won some games through luck and timely big plays. Now they were two thousand miles from campus, in a state with palm trees and beautiful girls, and by God, they could beat these bastards.

They were heavy underdogs, but they were ahead. The thought of winning, of beating this power, was too much to consider head-on. He held the idea gingerly, as though it were a welder's torch and without a mask he could only glance at it from the corners of his eyes.

The team was playing its game. The players had the odd ability to bring opponents down to their level, the way slow drivers can back up an entire freeway. Before the half he had been running near the sideline, and when he dived to make a tackle, he had been flipped somehow and then crushed in the pileup. His face went into the grass, his neck had been twisted, and he felt a searing jolt down one side. His eyes would not focus. He didn't know if he could move or not. He lay on the ground, stunned by the force that had overrun him. He had forgotten about that. He started to cry. He thought his neck had been snapped, but he was pretty sure it hadn't. Something just seemed unfair about all the force that had been applied to him. He said, "Mommy, mommy, mommy."

He remembered his buddy, the free safety who a few games ago had taken a knee flush on the temple and had then been carried off the field. The free safety had wept on the sidelines. When the defensive backs came off the field, they gathered around the doctor, who was asking the free safety what day it was and how many fingers he was holding up and who they were playing, and he gave all the correct answers, but he wouldn't stop crying. When they sat beside him, the free safety leaned forward and shook. "Don't make me like Cal," he said to each of them. "Don't make me like Cal." Cal was the stupidest player on the team.

He felt okay all of a sudden. The nerve pain had vanished. It wasn't serious. His eyes still didn't focus, but he gambled that the quarterback didn't know that and wouldn't work him. They ran a sweep the other way. But he felt slightly tentative now. The force had rocked him.

It was fourth and eight with less than a minute to play in the game, and they were still ahead. The powerful team had forty-seven yards to go to score a touchdown and win. A field goal wouldn't do it. The defensive backs talked to each other. He talked the loudest. The opponents were going for a first down. They needed to keep the ball. Don't give them eight yards. They want a fucking first down. Do you understand!

If they pick on me, I will do my job, he thought. They won't get a first down. If they do, my life will go on. No question about it. Don't give them a first down, he screamed again.

The strong safety was a short guy with a heavy beard. He was quiet and tough and sometimes when they'd come to practice he'd be lying on a training table with his ankles taped and full uniform on, sound asleep. He looked at the strong safety now and made a fist. The strong safety made one back.

The receivers all sprinted off the line. His hooked just past eight yards. Two other receivers did outs. The quarterback threw, but didn't. It was a pump-fake. The quarterback lofted the ball thirty yards downfield. The strong safety's man had hooked, too, then taken off again. The strong safety was beaten from here to east Jesus, because he wasn't giving up a first down.

The strong safety ran into the end zone behind his man and then dropped down as though shot. He lay there facedown without moving. He looked dead.

They watched the film of the game the next week, as usual. And every time they got to the end of the reel, the strong safety would drop face-first into the end-zone grass and lie there till the film ended.

It was quite a scene. He died again and again. Forever.

CHAPTER 7

There's Nothing We Can Do

Sometimes a person can sound mighty highfalutin when he starts dabbling in the realm of ethics and reform and ought-to-do, and that is as it should be. As somebody once wrote, let he who is without sin cast the first stone. And as someone else once noted, let those in glass houses be wary of throwing stones, at any time. But what makes the current state of big-time college football so enticing a target to anybody who can even grasp and weakly fling a pebble is that it is so *reformable*. I think that's why the whole thing makes me so mad. I am reminded of Oscar Wilde's final words as he lay dying in a cheap Paris hotel: ''My wallpaper and I are fighting a duel to the death. One or the other of us must go.'' That's college football and me.

All it will take to change the course of the sport is for university presidents to take a stand, to say that they are fed up with the current system and they will take it no more. They need the support of the school faculties and alumni and college football fans, but they can do it by themselves if they have enough courage. Sure, there will be casualties, but there are in any revolution. The point is that the presidents *do* have the power to bring about change; if they deny that, then they're not fit to hold their positions as custodians of our temples of knowledge. Way back in 1939, University of Chicago president Robert Maynard Hutchins up and abolished football at that football-loving school, and when asked why he replied simply, "To be successful, one must cheat. Everyone is cheating, and I refuse to cheat." No more and no less.

"Come on, you presidents," wrote former basketball coach and current TV announcer Al McGuire not long ago in the *NCAA News*. "Come out and say what you want. If you guys have the courage to say what shouldn't be, then it won't be. But it's time for you to take charge of your own destiny inside the jock world. No more shadowboxing in the Ivory Tower." If old Al recognizes the basic means to the solution, it can't be all that complicated; Al has said many times that he has instinct for certain on-court patterns and urban-based hustles, but that he's no genius.

The presidents and others involved—including the NCAA, the NFL, and big-time college football supporters—need a blueprint for reform, and I intend to provide that. To begin with, there are certain truths that everyone involved in the reform must admit, much the way alcoholics must admit certain things to themselves if they hope to be cured.

We must admit that:

- football started as an innocent student-run response to the repressiveness of the long-departed "collegiate way," and big-time sports' college connection is a perversion of that response.
- amateurism doesn't work and never will, except as a model for those who are not serious athletes or for whom sport is simply a pastime.
- high-level football players, like other elite athletes, are motivated by winning and will do everything they can to win.
- we love watching our favorite sports teams *win* and not just compete.

• we love the illusion of integrity brought by big-time college football's affiliation with the university world.

• education and big-time sport have nothing to do with one another. They are not mutually exclusive, but they are not necessarily related.

• being paid for playing a sport is not wrong, regardless of the age or educational background of the athlete. (Remember that fifteen-year-old tennis pros and uneducated hockey players deserve, and get, money for their efforts.)

• the game of football at its highest level has become too bizarre and dangerous to serve any educational function.

• just because we love the "illusion" of big-time college football, that is no reason to perpetuate fraud and corruption.

• the perversion of college athletics perverts all of us in subtle yet dangerous ways.

• the sport does not help the universities financially and may, in fact, detract from their economic health.

• the "good old days," if they were good (which seems unlikely), will not be back again. Nothing, my friends, comes back.

• sports are good and pleasurable and worthwhile even if they have nothing to do with college on the one hand and profit on the other.

Having admitted and accepted those truths, we—and particularly the presidents—should immediately take the following steps:

1. Establish a football league to be called the Age Group Professional Football League. The AGPFL will be analogous to the junior leagues that now exist in hockey, with some elements of baseball's minor leagues and the Continental Basketball Association.

2. Determine the Division I-A universities that want to retain big-time football and make them the nucleus of this league.

According to my guess, that will be anywhere from fifty to eighty schools from the PAC-10, the Western Athletic Conference, the Big Eight, the Big Ten, the ACC, the SEC, and the major independents. Certain currently "big-time" but academically oriented, athletically mediocre schools such as Rice, Northwestern, and Stanford may welcome the chance to bow out of the big time. The service academies should get out, too.

3. Request/demand the NFL's partial subsidy of the AGPFL, with the NFL guaranteeing a certain amount of money to be placed yearly in a pool for the AGPFL's use.

4. The players in the AGPFL need not be college students.

5. Use, when acceptable and appropriate, existing university facilities for member AGPFL teams. That would include locker rooms, practice fields, stadiums, etc.

6. AGPFL teams will also use the team colors and mascots of their sponsoring schools and will be prohibited by law from moving to another city or state.

7. To be eligible to play in the league a player must be at least eighteen years old and a high school graduate or have a high school equivalency diploma. Players can be no older than twenty-two.

8. Set up a reasonable pay scale for the players. Players may receive bonuses and contracts and all the other incentives typically given to pro athletes.

9. Set up a drug-testing program that follows the testing done in the NFL.

10. Universities that do not desire affiliation with the AGPFL may keep their football programs, but they may not charge admission to games or use their teams as money-making enterprises. Those teams that are not part of the AGPFL will be called "college football teams."

11. College football coaching staffs will be limited to four coaches, and all coaches must have other university teaching duties and be eligible for tenure.

12. A college player who improves his football skills and decides to try out for the AGPFL may join an AGPFL team, if there is one nearby and there is room on the roster and he is good enough to make the squad, while still remaining a student at his original college. Since there are no academic requirements in the AGPFL, the player will be judged solely as an employee by the league, and solely as a student by the school.

13. The college football season will be no more than eight games long, with single championship games allowed, but the entire season must start after school begins in the fall and end before Christmas break.

14. The AGPFL, on the other hard, will play a reasonable number of games, but no more than 75 percent of the total number played by the NFL.

15. Freshman will not be eligible to play on college football teams, though they may practice and play two or three games against other college freshmen.

16. There will be no spring practice in college football and no summer or fall practice before classes begin.

17. College football teams will be limited to five practices per week, with no practice lasting more than ninety minutes.

18. There will be no college athletic dorms.

19. Members of the AGPFL will receive one free year of education at the affiliated school for each year of service completed in the age group league. Players may redeem these scholarships at any time, even while playing in the AGPFL, though most likely the demands of the pro league would make class attendance difficult if not impossible during much of the school year. The players may redeem the scholarships only if they pass the entrance exam for the university. If they do not qualify for enrollment at the university, they may take remedial, non-degree-fulfilling courses instead of college courses. There will be no time limit on this offer; they can enroll right after the end of their football careers or ten years after or fifty years after.

20. College football players have only three years of eligibility after their freshman year. There will be no redshirting. No one over the age of twenty-two may play college football under any circumstances.

21. An intercollegiate governing board—the NCAA itself if it wants to hang around—will police the college football game. Board representatives will be composed of the presidents, athletic directors, and faculty members elected by the general faculty at each institution.

22. A school with an AGPFL team may not have another football team.

23. There will be no grants-in-aid or other university scholarships available to college football players that are not available to any and all students at the university.

24. College football coaches will not be allowed to make money from TV or radio shows or product endorsements. (These benefits will tend to remain in the big-time, the AGPFL, anyway.)

25. The college football program will be part of the university itself, coming under the same checks and balances, financial scrutiny, and academic review as the English and physics departments.

26. AGPFL teams may not sign players from college teams after either the AGPFL or college season has begun. College players may join AGPFL teams before the season begins, but they will most likely have to drop out of college to do so (for the reasons previously explained).

27. The NFL will draft from the AGPFL each year, but may not take AGPFL players once the AGPFL season has begun. There will be no calling-up of players during the season. AGPFL players will be eligible for the draft after one season; players drafted and cut by the NFL may return to their AGPFL team as long as they still meet the qualifications. College players may not be drafted until their eligibility is completed; staying in the college ranks is a declaration by the player that he does not want to turn pro or isn't ready to.

28. AGPFL teams will be owned by the universities, with

outside assistance if needed. The teams' primary functions will be to develop young football players, offer an exciting game to the public, and turn a profit. (Sound familiar?)

Now that the separate football leagues have been set up, let us examine what we have wrought. The benefits and ethical improvements of this new system are obvious.

There will no longer be any need for under-the-table payments to athletes since the AGPFL players are not amateurs. The college football players might still be seen as amateurs, but only because there is no reason or incentive to pay them. Moreover, the players who are big-time players in the Age Group Professional Football League—the members of the Oklahomas and Miamis and Alabamas, which will certainly want to play the big-time brand of ball—will now get fair compensation for their work as well as insurance and workmens' compensation in case of injury. There will no longer be any academic fraud because the young professional players have no grade or educational requirements whatsoever, just as players on the pro tennis tour have none. College football players will no longer be highly recruited, money-generating studs, and therefore should have no reason to get any breaks in the classroom even from football-mad professors.

There are no more autonomous athletic departments. The AGPFL exists to make money, which it should easily be able to do once it has the NFL subsidizing it and no more minor sports siphoning profits from its till. At last, young men who want to take a shot at being career football players, or who simply want to play at the highest level of the sport for a few years, but who don't care about college educations, have a place to play. Young men who want to be students and also play football may do so by playing college football, which will be similar to the level NCAA Division II and III schools play now. A good player who also is a serious student can try the AGPFL first and go to school later, much the way someone who tries to make it in a rock band or movie acting might come back to pursue an education.

There will no longer be any need for lying or hypocrisy by the football coaches. The AGPFL coaches won't have to think about education at all, and the college coaches will no longer be celebrities, but rather career college teachers who can afford to be concerned about their players' education.

If an AGPFL player finds he does not like the pro league or isn't good enough for it, he can drop out and go to college like a normal student. His risk of trying to play in the pro league does not guarantee him anything more than the scholarship credits he has accumulated. As for those who will wring their hands over the AGPFL dropouts who find themselves on the street with nothing to fall back on, they should be more concerned about the millions of American youths who drop out of high school with nothing to fall back on than a few young men who pursued dreams and fell short of attaining them. In the United States everybody has the freedom to fail.

Further, those who have played in the AGPFL will still have those credits to use for a real educational opportunity, a far better deal than they get now, when the opportunity given by a football scholarship on the one hand is taken away by the time-consuming demands of the sport on the other.

Fans of big-time college football can still root for the AGPFL teams, which will be much like the old big-time college teams except in attitude and compensation. The student-athlete label shouldn't matter much to a lot of fans, anyway, since many of them never went to college and their collegiate fandom is really only their latching onto an institution that offers them entertainment and vicarious status. The AGPFL should be able to provide those things, too. Other pluses are that students and professors will not have to accept the fraud of the phony student football player. Colleges no longer need to perpetuate a lie; they can become ethical and honorable places once again.

Schools may petition to move from college football to the

AGPFL if there is pressure to do so by students and faculty and alums. But once they move up, they must then drop their college team and have just the age group pro team. This will prevent college teams from acting as feeders to a school's AGPFL squad. Of course, AGPFL teams may drop out of the league and become college teams if they desire, but they must automatically begin working under the rules of the college game when they do so. Teams would be able to switch from one league to the other no more than once every four years, which would prevent their moving up and down to take advantage of team strengths or weaknesses or to otherwise manipulate the system.

Students may become much more interested in their college football teams once they see that the players really are students like themselves. Or they may find they love the pageantry and skill of the AGPFL. Either way, they will be seeing something that is fair and aboveboard.

Of course, there will be opponents to the plan. Big-time coaches and athletic directors and boosters may be outraged at the loss of jobs and the loss of clout they now have. But the AGPFL will accommodate many of those people, and the others can watch the college game or find new careers.

High school seniors will have to make a tougher decision about playing football than they currently do. They will have to decide whether to put off college for a while and try to make the big time in football or to cut back on the game and become real college students. But it's not that hard a decision, and there's plenty of time to recover if it's made incorrectly. After all, many other athletes, virtually all baseball players among them, have to make a similar decision when coming out of high school. And the prospect of going to college when one is older than other students is a minor drawback at best; college campuses are filled with students of all ages, and there would almost certainly be a cachet to getting one's education after time spent in the "manly" pro leagues.

Some fans may claim they don't get the same "rush" from supporting teams in the new leagues. Minor sports at universities may suffer financially at first until the universities acknowledge that those sports should be part of the school system itself and not dependent on the profits of a football juggernaut for their existence, or outside organizations—the AAU, U.S. Olympic Committee, etc.—pick up the slack and sponsor amateur teams for college-aged athletes. The NFL will bitch because it will have to pay for what it has always gotten for free—a steady supply of talent. And there are those boosters who will be unhappy about losing their trained pseudoamateur performers and the chance to revel in the illegal payments they made to those athletes, payments that somehow made the boosters feel important. To all those complaints I say, Too bad! Who cares? and Bravo! The gains here are much more important than the preservation of pleasures for people or institutions who have become comfortable with something that is wrong. What we're trying to do here, for once, is something that is just plain *right*.

Oh, my proposing this plan will probably have little or no effect on the powers that be in big-time college football. I am not foolish enough to think that my concerns mean very much to people who have a lot invested in the current system. Remember McCaskey's continuous-aiming-gun story?

That is why I have sounded off as loudly as I have. If we can't be goaded or reasoned into doing the right thing, maybe we can be shamed into it. Embarrassment may be as good a prod as logic. I hope it is.

I recently saw that Soviet Foreign Minister Eduard Shevardnadze was asked in an interview how he felt about sports. Shevardnadze smiled. "After we have eliminated all nuclear weapons, all chemical weapons," he said, "after we have substantially reduced conventional weapons so that they are within the limits of reasonable defensive sufficiently, after we have completed our *perestroika,* then we shall take up sports very seriously."

We are blessed here in this country to be able to take sports seriously right now. We owe something to that. We have the freedom in the face of that bounty to do something that will show future generations we cared. Not long ago my father-in-law gave me a transcript of the speech General George Patton delivered to him and other officers of the 4th Armored Division of the United States Army on the eve of the invasion of Normandy. Patton acknowledged the tremendous risk of the venture, but told the men that the invasion was as much an opportunity for them as it was a horror. "You can thank God that twenty years from now," Patton concluded, "when you're sitting around the fireside with your grandson on your knee and he asks what you did in this war—you won't have to shift to the other knee, cough, and say: 'I shoveled shit in Louisiana.' "

I've got nothing against Louisiana, and Patton probably didn't either, but the same choices he describes are the ones we can make now regarding college football. We can either stand up and fight, or grab a shovel and hang our heads for a long, long time.

STRETCHING

There had been a drought. The leaves on the trees clattered thinly in the hot puffs of wind, and the grass everywhere was yellow and dusty.

But the field was an oasis of green. The sprinklers had defined an oval that included the goalposts, the sidelines, and everything in between. As he bent far forward he could smell the grass. It smelled green. The color had become something special for him, a state of mind, an inducement to travel. He lay down in the grass and let the blades poke through his facemask.

He thought about the morning practice, about how he had been knocked out briefly, just for a second or two, in a tackling drill. At lunch he had eaten almost nothing, but he had drunk a gallon of lemonade. He weighed himself before the lemonade and then after, and he had gained seven pounds.

After lunch he and his roommate got into bed, turned on the air conditioner recently delivered by his roommate's concerned father, turned it on full-blast to squeeze every drop of moisture from the air, and squealed like pigs. Their legs were cramping, their necks were knotted, and they felt insane. The sheets were so cold and sweet that all they could do was giggle until the alarm clock rang.

And now he was tunnelling back into the grass. He discovered a bee, dead for some reason. From the drought? Do bees drink, he wondered. It was the size of a cow. On its back legs it carried saddlebags full of pollen, enough to make a vat of honey.

He wanted to drift forever, but he wanted to play the game, too. If only it wouldn't destroy him.

"All right!" a man yelled.

Here it came.

Afterword

As I sit here reading *The Hundred Yard Lie* six years after its initial printing, I am amazed at two things. First, it's hard for me to believe there really was that much crazy stuff going on in college football back then. And second, whew, was I angry about it.

I basically held true to my vow at the end of the book to stop covering big-time college football. I haven't written as much about boxing as I intended to (that was going to be my penance), but I've had quite a few things to say about pro football, the NBA, professional tennis, Major League Baseball, track and field, golf, Olympic sports, and other games. Because I've been out of the college football inner sanctum, however, I haven't seen the things I saw back when I was deep into the action.

But those things are still there.

I know that because I see them from the corners of my eyes, the way you notice fireflies on a summer night while driving down backroads in farm country. There was rap star Luther Campbell's 1995 letter to Miami city and county officials urging them to endorse a certain quarterback as the starter at the University of

Miami, or else. If his QB pick didn't get the job, the rapper concluded, he would "tell all" about wrongdoing in the Hurricanes' program and would organize a picket line for the Hurricanes' first home game. And Campbell's affiliation with the University of Miami? He had never been a student there, but he was, as the phrase goes, "a longtime Miami booster."

Much more would be revealed about the UM program, even without Campbell's assistance, leading *Sports Illustrated* to publish in the summer of 1995 a cover story urging the university's president, Tad Foote, to disband the team entirely, to get his school back to being a university first and a traveling sideshow second.

Beyond that, there was Heisman Trophy candidate Lawrence Phillips of the University of Nebraska pleading no contest to charges of assault and trespassing for beating up his former girlfriend, making him just one of four Cornhuskers from the 1994 and 1995 national championship teams to be arrested in the space of two months. Such troubles have led sportswriters and other handwringers to wonder if there is any connection between building a successful football program and lawlessness and rule breaking. If I were in my formerly sarcastic outrage mode, I could answer in one word: Duh.

But I'm not. I wrote this book and it speaks for me, so that I may remain calm and removed. I will, however, recite the facts regarding the last four national champions, preceding Nebraska, since we have already heard about the Cornhuskers' problems.

- University of Washington, 1990 champs: put on probation by the PAC 10 in 1993, with head coach Don James resigning under pressure from press and faculty.
- University of Miami, 1991 champs: still being investigated by the NCAA for so many rules violations that the death penalty may be recommended; former head coach Dennis Erickson quickly left following the 1994 season, without penalty, to become head coach of the NFL Seattle Seahawks.
- University of Alabama, 1992 champs: put on probation in the summer of 1995 for the first time in the school's history, following a three-year NCAA investigation.

• Florida State, 1993 champs: forced to suspend several players at the beginning of the 1994 season after they went on an agent-financed shopping spree at a Tallahassee sporting goods store.

Sports Illustrated's 1995 preseason number one pick, the University of Southern California, has also had its share of problems. During the season, several Trojan players were suspended from the team for allegedly taking money and gifts from a sports agent, and star wide receiver Keyshawn Johnson is still under investigation by NCAA authorities who are trying to determine whether he received cash from an agent while in junior college.

None of this is new turf for head coach John Robinson, who led the Trojans from 1976 to 1982, went on to the NFL, and then returned to USC in 1993. During Robinson's first tenure, Southern Cal won three Rose Bowls and one national championship, but it also got hit with several years of NCAA probation for a variety of ticket-scalping and academic scams. Such negatives, it would seem, are just part of the Robinson style of leadership. Or else they're inherent to the University of Southern California football program—or the college football system in general.

Regardless, head coaches who can guarantee wins are more in demand than ever. Florida State's Bobby Bowden, already one of the highest-paid coaches in the nation, entered new territory when he received a five-year deal from the school and its boosters that reportedly will pay him $1 million annually. The seven-figure fee is made possible in part by the corporate sponsorships that help fund the FSU football program. Such sponsorships are now so common that when the University of Colorado recently signed a five-year deal for $5.6 million with Nike to equip the school's athletes with Nike apparel, the announcement barely made the fine print in the notes columns of the nation's sports pages.

Consider too the strange plight of a walk-on football player at the University of Kentucky. His name is Harold Dennis, and he is not a particularly gifted athlete, but he is a remarkable human being. Horribly burned on his face and chest in a drunk driver auto accident when he was just a boy, Dennis has become a champion of perseverance and resilience, refusing to let his disfigurement stop him from leading a productive and exciting life.

But when Dennis signed a contract with a Los Angeles talent agency, giving the company the right to shop a movie script based on his inspirational life—a script written by a U.K. history professor, no less—the NCAA cracked down. Dennis had to tear up the contract to remain eligible to play football at Kentucky. He was forced to do this because the deal breached the NCAA's amateurism clause, even though Dennis had received no money for signing the deal and would receive none until the movie was shot, which likely would occur long after his eligibility had expired, if at all.

No matter that the Kentucky head football coach, Bill Curry, makes good money to coach a team that went 1-10 in 1994 and 4-7 in 1995, or that Kentucky basketball coach Rick Pitino makes a million dollars a year. Rules are rules.

When I talked to NCAA spokesperson Kathryn Reith about the Dennis dilemma—a young man unable to pursue a business venture because the NCAA did not allow its athletes to profit from sports participation—she agreed that it was unfortunate in this case. But then she added, "Member institutions have said, 'We think the players should be amateurs.'"

And why not? Having the ability to determine the financial status of its athletes is perhaps the NCAA's greatest power. And the world is yet waiting for the first ruling cartel that arbitrarily decides its workers are underpaid—or, if unpaid, that they should be paid at all.

It's amusing, really, the accomplices you pick up in life. Walter Byers, founding father of the NCAA and the secretive, conservative, and dictatorial executive director who ruled that organization with a steel fist for thirty-six years until stepping down in 1987, is now professing the same credo that I am.

More than any other man, Byers is the one who made college football the modern, hypocritical juggernaut it is. And yet, now that he has retired from running the machine, he is singing a very new song. The NCAA, he writes in his new book *Unsportsmanlike Conduct: Exploiting College Athletes,* is "overrun by the pervasive influence of big money, national publicity and entertainment excitement." The players are powerless servants, he continues, exploited by coaches, NCAA officials, and other "industry plutocrats." Amateurism, he declares, is at the root of the problem: "The colleges have expanded their control of athletes in the name of amateurism—a modern-day misnomer for economic tyranny."

I'm not sure even I was that blunt. Well, yes I was. And I suppose I'm pleased to have a man of Byers's historic influence on my side. But another part of me is a bit disturbed by the man's turnabout. Where, Mr. Byers, was your conscience when the things you did mattered?

One of the main reasons I wrote this book with such a sense of high indignation is because I knew from my research that almost everything I was going to say had been said before. And nobody listened. Maybe, I figured, if I screamed louder than anybody else, a few folks would hear me.

• • •

I recently found the time to read a book on college football that I've been meaning to read for quite awhile, and I'd like to quote some random passages from it:

> College football today is one of the last great strongholds of genuine old-fashioned American hypocrisy.
>
> There are occasionally abortive attempts to turn football into an honest woman [*sic*], but, to date, the fine old game that interests and entertains literally millions of people has managed to withstand these insidious attacks.
>
> Kids, goodness knows, are dumb, but not so dumb they don't know what is going on. It is a curious thing that the college to which a boy goes, not only for an education, but for the set of morals, ethics, and ideals with which to carry on in later life, is the first place he learns

> beyond any question of doubt that you can get away with murder if you don't get caught at it or if you know the right people when you do get nabbed. His university is playing a dirty, lying game and it doesn't take him very long to find it out.
>
> If there is anything good about college football it is the fact that it seems to bring entertainment, distraction, and pleasure to many millions of people. But the price, the sacrifice to decency, I maintain, is too high.

The book is entitled *Farewell to Sport,* and it was written by the noted sportswriter Paul Gallico. In 1938.

• • •

But who knows? Maybe this time people will hear. As every football coach I ever had told me, you never know unless you try.

—Rick Telander
Chicago, Ill.

Acknowledgments

In the writing of this book I have borrowed freely from the knowledge of others. There are hundreds of people I should thank, and I hope they know who they are. I must give a special bow to Tommy Chaikin, Professor James Frey, Bob Goldman, John Hoberman, Leonard Koppett, Ron Smith, Lois Wallace, Rik Warch, and James Weeks.

Mark Mulvoy and Peter Carry have been more generous and understanding of my idiosyncrasies than they had any right to be. Rob Fleder has helped from the start.

Most of all, I thank Jeff Neuman, my editor at Simon and Schuster. Without him, there would be no book, only confusion. Because of him, I am purged.

RICK TELANDER is the lead sports columnist for the *Chicago Sun-Times,* a special contributor to *Sports Illustrated,* and a member of "The Sportswriters on TV," seen weekly on Sports Channel America and other cable affiliates. He has taught English literature and journalism at Northwestern University, his alma mater, where he swam and played football. A second-team All Big Ten cornerback at Northwestern, he was twice named an Academic All Big Ten. His other books include *Heaven Is a Playground,* about inner-city boys' basketball, and *From Red Ink to Roses,* about the financial and athletic workings of the University of Wisconsin at Madison.

MURRAY SPERBER is an associate professor of English and American studies at Indiana University.

RICHARD WARCH is the president of Lawrence University in Appleton, Wisconsin.